d-day 1944

omaha beach

STEVEN J ZALOGA

d-day 1944

omaha beach

Praeger Illustrated Military History Series

PRAEGER

Westport, Connecticut
London

Library of Congress Cataloging-in-Publication Data

Zaloga, Steve.
    D-Day 1944: Omaha Beach / Steven J. Zaloga.
        p. cm – (Praeger illustrated military history, ISSN 1547-206X)
    Originally published: Oxford: Osprey, 2003.
    Includes bibliographical references and index.
    ISBN 0-275-98266-1 (alk. paper)
    1. World War, 1939–1945 – Campaigns – France – Normandy. 2. Normandy (France) –
    History, Military – 20th century. I. Title. II. Series.
    D756.5.N6Z35   2004
    940.54'2142–dc22 2003063210

British Library Cataloguing in Publication Data is available.

First published in paperback in 2003 by Osprey Publishing Limited, Elms Court,
Chapel Way, Botley, Oxford OX2 9LP. All rights reserved.

Copyright © 2004 by Osprey Publishing Limited

Library of Congress Catalog Card Number: 2003063210
ISBN: 0-275-98266-1
ISSN: 1547-206X

Praeger Publishers, 88 Post Road West, Westport, CT 06881
An imprint of Greenwood Publishing Group, Inc.
www.praeger.com

Printed in China through World Print Ltd.

The paper used in this book complies with the Permanent Paper Standard issued
by the National Information Standards Organization (Z39.48-1984).

10 9 8 7 6 5 4 3 2 1

ILLUSTRATED BY: Howard Gerrard

CONTENTS

INTRODUCTION   7

CHRONOLOGY   12

OPPOSING COMMANDERS   13

German commanders • American commanders

OPPOSING PLANS   21

The American plan • The German plan

OPPOSING ARMIES   36

German forces • American forces

D-DAY   42

The first assault wave, 0530–0700hrs • The second assault wave, 0700–0800hrs

Stalemate on the beach • The Rangers at Pointe-du-Hoc

Consolidating the beachhead • The battles for the villages

OMAHA BEACH IN RETROSPECT   87

THE BATTLEFIELD TODAY   92

FURTHER READING   94

INDEX   95

KEY TO MILITARY SYMBOLS

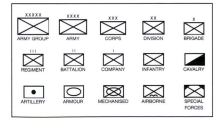

D-Day at Omaha Beach as seen by a Coast Guard photographer on an LCVP landing troops of 1/16th Infantry on Easy Red beach. The tank in the foreground is A-9, one of the few M4A1 tanks from the ill-fated 741st Tank Battalion to make it ashore. (NARA)

INTRODUCTION

Of the landings on the five assault beaches in Normandy on D-Day, Omaha Beach was the only one ever in doubt. Within moments of landing, a third of the assault troops in the first wave were casualties. The difficulties encountered on "bloody Omaha" were due to the more difficult terrain on this coastline, the unexpected presence of a first-rate German division at the beach and inadequate fire support. Yet in spite of all these problems, by the end of D-Day, the Atlantic Wall had been breached and the US Army's V Corps was firmly entrenched on the French coast.

THE STRATEGIC SITUATION

The Allied planning to assault Fortress Europe had been under way since 1942 and the Overlord plan began to take shape in 1943. Winston Churchill argued for a traditional maritime strategy of peripheral attack through Italy and the Balkans, but US military commanders and many senior British commanders favored a direct attack on Germany by the most plausible route, through northern France. The most significant disagreement concerned the US intent to stage two amphibious assaults, Operation Neptune in northwestern France, and Operation Anvil through the French Mediterranean coast. Churchill and many senior British commanders were firmly opposed to the southern France assault, realizing it would drain momentum from the Italian theater. With British

There was no more vivid symbol of the Atlantic Wall than the heavy coastal guns of the Kriegsmarine along the Channel coast like this one at Le Havre. These batteries were in their densest concentration on the Pas de Calais where the Wehrmacht expected the Allies to land. (NARA)

GERMAN FORCES IN THE GRANDCAMPS SECTOR, 6 JUNE 1944

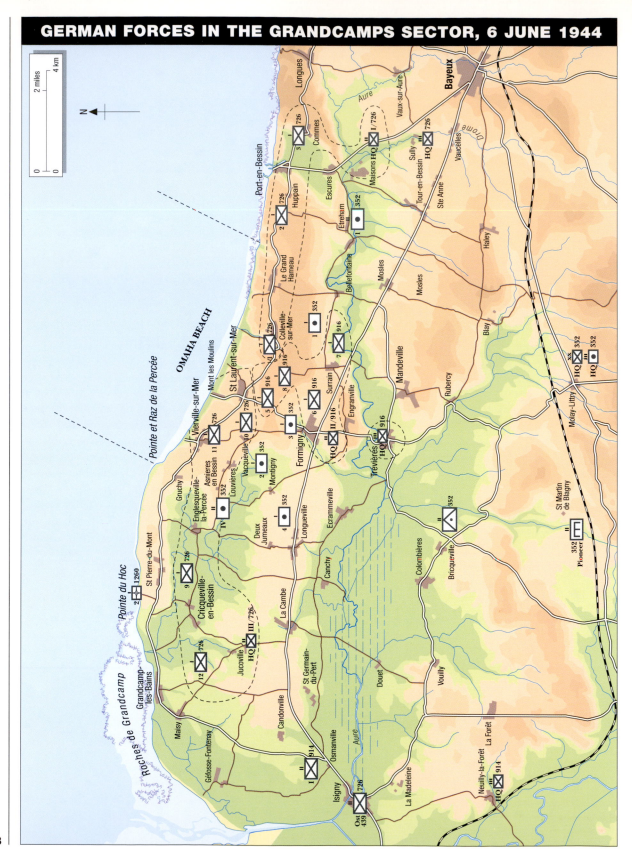

Omaha Beach, known to the Germans as the Grandcamps sector, was 7,000 yards long. This view from east to west shows the E-3 Colleville draw in the foreground and the Pointe-et-Raz-de-la-Percée towards the top. (MHI)

manpower reserves at breaking point and the US Army expected to provide the majority of forces for operations in France, Britain was losing its role as the senior partner in the Allied coalition. The American strategic viewpoint prevailed, although the more experienced British staffs shaped the actual planning for Neptune. In spite of significant controversies, not only between the Americans and the British, but among the combat services of both countries, the Allied coalition remained focused on its shared goal of defeating Germany. The Anglo-American partnership proved to be remarkably resilient in submerging national and service differences when they interfered with the mission.

One of the initial dilemmas was the target for Operation Neptune. The Pas de Calais opposite Dover was the narrowest point of the English Channel and had the added advantage of being closer to the expected route into Germany, through the Low Countries and across the northern Rhine plains. It was also the most obvious target and the area that the Germans were most diligently fortifying in 1943. Normandy was the next most likely area since the Bay of the Seine offered some shelter from weather and there were sufficient beaches with characteristics suitable for amphibious assault. Although more distant from the ultimate objective, Normandy was also less likely to attract the type of heavy defenses the Germans were constructing in the Pas de Calais. The problem in the invasion area was the lack of ports like Le Havre or Calais, but British naval planners had already begun to develop an ingenious artificial harbor that could provide a logistical base until neighboring ports such as Cherbourg were seized. The first draft of the Overlord plan was completed in July 1943, and approved by the Combined Joint Chiefs of Staff in August. Under the plan Operation Neptune would take place in May 1944 and Operation Anvil would follow as soon as it was possible to shift the necessary naval amphibious forces from the English Channel to the Mediterranean.

Overlord consisted of four phases. Operation Pointblank was already under way by the USAAF and RAF aimed at gaining air superiority over the future battlefield by destroying the Luftwaffe and crippling its ability to manufacture, maintain, and fuel its aircraft. The other element of the first phase was an attempt to deceive the Germans about the location of the actual landing site, Operation Fortitude. The second preparatory phase was aimed at isolating the battlefield by air attacks against communication centers, and road and rail networks that linked the Normandy area to reinforcements. Since air attacks limited to Normandy would give away the location of the planned invasion, more missions were actually flown against the Pas de Calais, as part of an effort to reinforce the Operation Fortitude deception. The third phase was Operation Neptune itself, the amphibious landings in Normandy. The fourth phase was the follow-up and build-up phase, aimed at reinforcing the bridgehead in preparation for the campaign in France.

The German view of the invasion beaches in Normandy. In the foreground are two rows of barbed wire, while in the surf are several rows of stakes, usually topped with Teller anti-tank mines. (MHI)

The preparatory work for Overlord took place in the shadow of the failed Dieppe raid of 1942[1]. Dieppe underscored how risky amphibious operations would be against a defended shoreline, but it also provided useful lessons. By 1944 the Allies had further amphibious experience including the landings in North Africa in November 1942 and the Sicily, Salerno, and Anzio landings in Italy in 1943–44. Neptune presented problems beyond the Italian experiences since it would involve landing against a fortified beach, while the previous landings had been conducted against uncontested and largely unprotected beaches. These challenges prompted the development of a host of new innovations such as the artificial harbors, new types of landing craft and assault vessels, specialized armored vehicles, and novel engineer equipment to overcome obstacles.

From the German perspective 1944 was the year of decision. The Wehrmacht had lost the strategic initiative in 1943 following its failed summer offensive at Kursk and the Allied offensive in Italy. Hitler believed that a stout defense in 1944 would lead to cracks in the Allied coalition that might provide the Wehrmacht with opportunities to reverse Germany's declining fortunes on the battlefield. The defeat of an Allied landing attempt in France was a prime opportunity. Hitler's strategic outlook was colored by his experience as a soldier in World War I, where there was no higher objective than the stalwart defense of every last inch of ground. By the beginning of 1944, German forces were scattered all over Europe from Norway and Finland in the north to Greece and the Balkans in the south, and from the Channel Islands in the west to the steppes of Ukraine in the east. "Who defends everything, defends nothing" is a military adage that Hitler ignored at Germany's peril. The Wehrmacht was stretched thin everywhere and Hitler rebuffed attempts to pull troops out of the peripheries to reinforce the most vital sectors. He took ill-advised comfort in the bloated Wehrmacht order of battle, ignoring that it had become a hollow force.

Bled white by the precarious situation on the Eastern Front, the Wehrmacht's innovative traditions in the art of war had stagnated and been overtaken by the Allies' more advanced approach. While some senior

1 See Campaign 127: *Dieppe 1942 – Prelude to D-Day*

German commanders who had fought Britain and the United States had some appreciation of the new style of deep battle, most did not. The Anglo-American style of war emphasized the use of airpower both as a third dimension in the land battle and as a means to deepen the battlefield. At the strategic level, long-range bombers weakened the military might of Germany by attacking its military industries, fuel production, and infrastructure. At the operational level, Allied medium bombers isolated the battlefield by destroying the road and rail networks feeding the forward edge of battle, sapping the Wehrmacht of its mobility and preventing reinforcement. At the tactical level, fighter-bombers outflanked ground formations from the air, extended the firepower of the Allies beyond the range of traditional artillery and disrupted the conduct of Wehrmacht operations with their ability to strike unexpectedly practically anytime, anywhere. The decay of the Luftwaffe undermined attempts to resist the forthcoming invasion of France. Rommel grimly noted that, "even with the most modern weapons, anyone who has to fight against an enemy in complete control of the air, fights like a savage against modern European troops, under the same handicaps and with the same chance of success."

The decline of the Luftwaffe also helped blind German intelligence to the Allied build-up in the ports of southern England facing Normandy. Photo reconnaissance missions over Britain were almost impossible and only two photos of British ports were obtained in the spring of 1944. Other intelligence means proved even more dangerous to German strategy as British counter-intelligence had managed to capture every agent dropped into Britain and had turned many into double agents. Berlin was fed a string of false reports reinforcing their mistaken beliefs about the invasion focus on the Pas de Calais and Picardy coastlines. The British success in breaking the German Enigma codes provided a vital source of information on German activities, but a most dangerous security breach was the US decryption of the code used by the Japanese embassy in Berlin. Ambassador Oshima Hiroshi reported on his frequent meetings with senior Nazi leaders, providing not only insight into Hitler's strategic views, but details of German dispositions such as his November 1943 inspection tour of German defenses on the French coast. The failures of German intelligence and counter-intelligence left the senior German leadership blind while at the same time exposing a remarkably complete picture of German plans to the Allies.

The consensus among German military leaders was that the main attacks would take place against the Pas de Calais or Picardy coast. The landings at Anzio on 22 January 1944 led a growing number of German commanders to believe that the Allies would launch several smaller amphibious attacks to draw off German reserves from the main landing. This greatly confused German defense plans and restricted the actions of German theater commanders because Berlin was increasingly unwilling to commit any reserves until it was evident that an Allied landing was in fact a major operation and not merely another diversion.

CHRONOLOGY

July 1943 First draft of Overlord plan completed

August 1943 Overlord plan approved by Combined Joint Chiefs of Staff

3 November 1943 Führer Directive 51 gives priority to reinforcing Western Front

6 November 1943 Rommel appointed to lead Army Group for Special Employment

4 June 1944 Poor weather forces cancellation of attack on Monday 5 June 1944

5 June 1944 Eisenhower decides that weather will permit execution of Neptune on 6 June 1944

Tuesday 6 June 1944 D-Day

  0030hrs Minesweepers clear channel to beachhead

  0100hrs German units alerted due to reports of Allied paratroopers

  0300hrs Task Force O arrives off Omaha Beach, anchors 25,000 yards from beach

  0310hrs General Marcks orders 84th Corps reserves, Kampfgruppe Meyer, to move to junction between Omaha and Utah beach to deal with paratroopers

  0415hrs Troops from assault waves begin loading in landing craft

  0530hrs DD tanks begin swim to beach

  0545hrs Naval bombardment group begins shelling Omaha Beach; firing ends at 0625

  0629hrs First wave of tanks begins landing

  0631hrs First wave of assault troops and Gap Assault Teams begins landing

  0700hrs Tide turns, obstacles gradually submerged by 0800

  0700–0730hrs Second wave of troops land

  0710hrs Rangers arrive at Pointe-du-Hoc 40 minutes late; reach summit by 0725

  0720hrs First advance over the bluffs by group under Lt Spalding, E/16th Infantry

  0750hrs Advance over the bluffs begins by 116th Infantry led by Gen Cota and Col Canham

  0800hrs Admiral Bryant orders destroyers to close on beach to provide fire support

  0810hrs Advance by 5th Rangers over the bluffs begins

  0820hrs Regimental HQ of 16th RCT lands, Col Taylor begins rallying troops

  0830hrs Beachmaster orders no further vehicles to be landed at Omaha due to congestion

  0835hrs General Kraiss directs Kampfgruppe Meyer to stop British advance from Gold Beach except for one battalion aimed at the Colleville penetration

  0900hrs WN60 strongpoint falls to L/16th Infantry

  0915hrs WN70 strongpoint abandoned due to advance by Cota's force on Vierville

  1000hrs 18th Infantry and 115th Infantry move towards beach in LCIs, they are delayed by lack of clear lanes

  1100hrs LCI-554 and LCT-30 force their way through to the beach, restoring momentum to the landings

  1130hrs E-1 St Laurent draw opened; first exit cleared on D-Day

  1300hrs Hour-long naval bombardment of D-1 Vierville draw concludes; survivors surrender

  1300hrs Engineers complete makeshift road over bluff near E-1 St Laurent draw; vehicle assembly area completed by 1500hrs

  1335hrs Kraiss reports to 84th Corps HQ that invasion force stopped except at Colleville

  1630hrs E-3 Colleville draw finally taken

  1700hrs Tanks begin moving through E-1 St Laurent draw

  1800hrs D-1 Vierville draw finally opened by engineers

  1825hrs Kraiss orders 1/GR.914 to retake Pointe-du-Hoc

  2000hrs D-3 Les Moulins draw declared open

  2000hrs Engineers begin clearing path through E-3 Colleville draw, opens at 0100 on D+1

OPPOSING COMMANDERS

GERMAN COMMANDERS

The Byzantine dynamics of the Nazi political leadership undermined German capabilities to defeat the forthcoming invasion. By 1944 Hitler had lost confidence in the Wehrmacht commanders and had continued to usurp more and more of the decision-making down to the tactical level. Hitler's meddling was erratic and unpredictable and his lazy and disorganized leadership style encouraged the formation of competing factions in the military and the government. This was all too evident in the failed attempts to create a unified command in France where not only was there the usual inter-service rivalries between the navy, army, and air force, but also the Waffen-SS and the Organization Todt paramilitary construction service. The armed forces high command (OKW) headed by Generalfeldmarschall Wilhelm Keitel was a nominal joint staff but in fact the Luftwaffe and navy were represented by junior officers, and Reichsmarschall Hermann Göring and Admiral Raeder circumvented the OKW when it suited them.

The commander in chief in the West (OB West) from March 1942 was **Generalfeldmarschall Gerd von Rundstedt**. The revered victor of the 1940 Battle of France was described by one of his Panzer commanders as "an elderly man … a soldier of thorough training with adequate experience in practical warfare, but without an understanding of a three-dimensional war involving the combined operations of the Heer [army], Kriegsmarine [navy] and Luftwaffe. He was a gentleman and had the personal confidence and respect of his subordinate commanders and his troops. His authority was limited and quite handicapped. His chief of staff [Blumentritt] was not a suitable complement, either as to capability or character." A post-war US Army study concluded that the lack of unified command in France was a more serious weakness than shortages of troops and equipment.

Workers from Organization Todt scramble for cover as a US P-38 Lightning reconnaissance aircraft piloted by Lt Albert Lanker makes a fast pass over the Normandy beaches on 6 May 1944, a month before the landings. The German construction teams continued to install more anti-invasion obstacles on the beaches until D-Day. (NARA)

While Rundstedt commanded army units, **Generalfeldmarschall Hugo Sperrle** was in charge of Luftflotte 3 including 3rd Flak Korps, and the Luftwaffe paratroop and field divisions. **Admiral Theodor Krancke** commanded Navy Group West along the French coast, including the coastal artillery batteries that would shift to army jurisdiction only after the invasion had begun. German security troops being used for occupation duty were under the control of the two military governors. Tactical control was supposed to shift to OB West once the invasion started, but the disjointed command before the invasion hampered coordinated preparation of defenses and complicated control of the forces during the critical first hours of the invasion.

Rundstedt's limited control was evident in the construction of the Atlantic Wall, a series of coastal fortifications started on Hitler's insistence after the St Nazaire and Dieppe raids of 1942. The fortifications were the responsibility of the Organization Todt paramilitary construction force, which reported to armament minister Albert Speer, not to the army. Furthermore, the navy was responsible for most of the fortified coastal guns, which were positioned as they saw fit. Army artillery officers derided them as "battleships of the dunes," located on the coast vulnerable to Allied bombardment instead of being sheltered further to the rear. Hitler wanted 15,000 concrete strongpoints manned by 300,000 troops by May 1943 – an impossible target. The focus was on the Pas de Calais and in the summer of 1943 further emphasis was placed on this sector due to Hitler's decision to locate the new V-1 and V-2 missile bases in this area. In spite of the rhetoric about an impregnable "Fortress Europe", the poor state of defenses prompted Rundstedt to send a special report to Hitler in October 1943, which led to Führer Directive 51 on 3 November 1943. This reversed former priorities and recognized the need to strengthen defenses in the West in view of the likelihood of a 1944 Allied attack. The most tangible outcome of this debate was the assignment of **Generalfeldmarschall Erwin Rommel** to head the newly created Army Group for Special Employment (later Army Group B), a post directly under OKW for direction of the invasion front.

Rommel's new post partly duplicated Rundstedt's, but both officers attempted to make the best of a confused situation. Rommel's first activities involved an inspection of the Atlantic Wall construction and he invigorated the effort in previously neglected sectors such as Normandy and Brittany. Rommel's appointment brought to a head the debate about the deployment of forces to repel the expected invasion. Rommel argued that the invasion had to be stopped cold on the beaches. It was, therefore, essential that reserves, especially the Panzers, be kept close enough to the beaches for them to intervene promptly. The commander of Panzer Gruppe West, **General Leo Freiherr Geyr von Schweppenburg** argued vociferously that the Panzer divisions and the Luftwaffe should be held back from the coastal zone and kept in reserve to form a counter-attack force that would strike after the Allies had landed. Geyr cited the examples of Sicily, Salerno, and Anzio, where German Panzer forces committed to the coastal battle had been stopped by heavy naval gunfire. Geyr argued that the landings could not be stopped, and that the beach defenses should only be an economy-of-force effort – enough to significantly delay and disrupt but not so much as to drain forces from the decisive battle inland. Rommel retorted that, given Allied air superiority, the Panzers would never be able to mass for a counter-attack and to permit the Allies to win a firm lodgment ensured disaster. The matter came to a head in March 1944 when Rommel asked Hitler for expanded powers to unify the command under his control. Hitler agreed to a compromise, putting three of Geyr's Panzer divisions under Rommel's operational control as the Army Group B reserve, but leaving three other Panzer divisions under Rundstedt's OB West command and the remaining four under direct OKW control as strategic reserves. As a result, the German strategy for Normandy remained a jumble of Rommel's scheme for an immediate defense of the beach and Rundstedt/Geyr's plans for a decisive battle after the landings. On D-Day Rommel was in Germany, hoping to persuade Hitler to give him control of more Panzer divisions.

German forces in Normandy were part of the Seventh Army, which controlled German army units on the neighboring Cotentin peninsula and Brittany as well. The Seventh Army was commanded by **Generaloberst Friedrich Dollman**. He had won the Iron Cross in World War I, commanded a corps in Poland and the Seventh Army in the battle of France in 1940. While he was a highly competent officer, he spent most of the war on occupation duty and many battle-hardened veterans of the Eastern Front were skeptical that his staff was up to the task. Dollman died of a heart attack on 28 June 1944, less than a month after D-Day.

The Normandy sector was the responsibility of the 84th Infantry Corps commanded by **General der Infanterie Erich Marcks**. He was widely regarded as one of the best general staff officers and served early in the war with an army corps in Poland, and with the 18th Army in France in 1940. He was involved in the planning for Operation Barbarossa, and commanded the 101st Jäger Division at the time of the invasion of the Soviet Union in 1941. After he lost a leg in combat in March 1942, he was reassigned to the command of the 337th Infantry Division following his recuperation. His skills as a divisional commander led to his elevation to army corps command, first the 66th Corps in

The commander of the 352nd Infantry Division defending Omaha Beach was Generalleutnant Dietrich Kraiss. (NARA)

September 1942, then the 87th Corps. The Nazis considered him politically suspect as he had been an aide to General von Schleicher, murdered by the SS in 1934, and he was passed over by Hitler for army command. Instead, he was assigned to the 84th Corps in France on 1 August 1943 as part of the process to refresh the command structure in France with Eastern Front veterans. Marcks did not agree with Rommel over tactics to defeat an amphibious landing since he felt that his corps was far too weak and thinly spread to defend the extensive coastline it had been assigned. He favored the construction of a string of field fortifications in modest depth, but relying on a corps reserve of mobile infantry and Panzers within a day's march of the coast to carry out the burden of the defense. Due to the expected bad weather, the Seventh Army had scheduled a series of anti-invasion staff exercises for senior commanders in Rennes for 6 June, with Marcks assigned the role of the senior Allied commander. At 0100hrs on 6 June as the Allied paratroopers were approaching their objectives, Marcks was celebrating his birthday with his staff at St Lô, planning to depart a few hours later for Rennes. He was killed in Normandy during an air attack on 12 June 1944.

The 352nd Infantry Division, commanded by **Generalleutnant Dietrich Kraiss**, defended Omaha Beach. He was a professional soldier, commissioned into the 126th Infantry Regiment in 1909 at the age of 20, and fought in World War I. At the outbreak of World War II he was commander of the 90th Infantry Regiment. His successful leadership in the early campaigns resulted in his appointment to command the 168th Infantry Division in Russia on 8 July 1941, which he led until March 1943. He was transferred to the newly formed 355th Infantry Division, which he commanded until it was disbanded on 6 November 1943 due to the heavy losses it had suffered during the autumn fighting in Russia. Kraiss was then transferred to France to command the newly formed 352nd Infantry Division which was originally earmarked for the Eastern Front. He was wounded during the fighting near St Lô on 2 August 1944, dying of his wounds four days later.

AMERICAN COMMANDERS

General Dwight D. Eisenhower was assigned to command the Supreme Headquarters Allied Expeditionary Force (SHAEF) in December 1943. Eisenhower had served as aide to General Douglas MacArthur in the Philippines in the years leading up to World War II, an invaluable education in the lessons of coalition building and the impact of politics on military planning. Although he was assigned to a regimental command on his return to the US in 1940, his reputation as one of the army's rising stars led the War Department to transfer him to War Plans in Washington. His performance as the chief of staff of the Third Army in the Louisiana maneuvers in the autumn of 1941 caught the attention of the army's chief of staff, George C. Marshall, and ignited his meteoric rise. Eisenhower played a central role in strategic decision making during the early years of the war, and was put in command of US forces for the amphibious landings in North Africa 1942. In contrast to the disjointed German command structure, the Allied command structure was far more centralized. One of

Senior commanders of the US forces off Omaha are seen here on the bridge of the cruiser USS *Augusta* on 8 June 1944. In the foreground is Rear Admiral Alan Kirk, commander of the Western Naval Task Force, Major General Omar Bradley, commander of the First US Army, Rear Admiral A.D. Struble, and General Ralph Royce of the Ninth Tactical Air Force. (NARA)

the first challenges to Eisenhower's authority was the resistance of senior US Army Air Force generals to the diversion of their long-range bombers from their strategic missions against Germany to the tactical operations to isolate the battlefield in France prior to D-Day. Although his critics have pointed to Eisenhower's lack of tactical battlefield experience, his visionary views on combined arms warfare as well as his astute political skills made him an ideal commander for a coalition force depending on tri-service cooperation by two Allied armed forces.

The tactical commander of the US Army in Overlord was **Lieutenant General Omar Bradley**, commander of the First US Army. Bradley had been a classmate of Eisenhower's at the US Military Academy at West Point in the class of 1915. Bradley's performance at the infantry school

Commander of the 1st Infantry Division was Major General Clarence Huebner, seen here briefing General Dwight Eisenhower and General Omar Bradley a few weeks after D-Day during the operations near Cherbourg. (NARA)

in the early 1930s and his work on the General Staff in 1938 attracted Marshall's attention. Bradley raised the new 82nd Division that would later fight as an airborne division in Normandy, and afterwards became deputy commander of George S. Patton's II Corps in the North African campaign. Marshall favored intelligent, conservative planners like Bradley over charismatic leaders like Patton for senior commands and Bradley received the nod to lead First US Army in August 1943.

The force assaulting Omaha Beach came from V Corps, led by **Major General Leonard Gerow**. He was older than either Eisenhower or Bradley, Virginia Military Institute class of 1911, and commanded Eisenhower in 1941 while heading the War Plans division of the general staff. Gerow was regarded by many as the quintessential staff officer, comfortable with planning combat operations but not leading them. Patton despised him, calling him one of the most mediocre corps commanders in Europe and later calling his appointment to head the War College after the war "a joke". But Gerow had Marshall's and Eisenhower's confidence, and was given command of the corps in July 1943 after having led the 29th Division. Bradley had brought in more experienced corps commanders from other theaters, including J. Lawton "Lightning Joe" Collins from the Pacific, to lead at neighboring Utah Beach and probably would not have chosen Gerow had the choice been his. But with his V Corps the first US tactical formation in the UK and with the support of Eisenhower, Gerow would lead the attack. Gerow locked horns with Bradley over many details of the Omaha Beach assault plans and several of his improvements would later prove vital in the success of the operation.

Senior US commanders wanted an experienced unit to land at Omaha Beach and, not surprisingly, the "Big Red One" 1st Infantry Division was selected. Led by the charismatic General Terry Allen and Theodore Roosevelt in North Africa and Sicily, the division had developed a cocksure reputation. Their popular definition of the US Army was "the Big Red One and a million frigging replacements." Bradley relieved the popular Allen on Sicily in August 1943, replacing him with **Major General Clarence Huebner**. Huebner was a veteran of the 1st Division in World War I,

awarded the Distinguished Service Medal for his courageous and skilled leadership of the 28th Infantry. Huebner, a strict disciplinarian, had a hard time asserting control after Allen was sacked. He imposed a strict training regime on the division when transferred to Britain and the rambunctious unit was finally won over. Huebner would later command V Corps under Patton in Germany in 1945.

The second Omaha Beach division, 29th Infantry Division, had been commanded by Gerow until July 1943 when he was replaced by West Pointer and former cavalry officer **Major General Charles Gerhardt**. He had been commissioned in 1917 and served on the staff of the 89th Division in World War I. Gerhardt's excellent performance as a cavalry brigade commander in the 1941 Louisiana maneuvers prompted Marshall to give him command of the new 91st Division. Gerhardt was a very traditional officer demanding a high level of discipline. His stern leadership of the 29th Division helped overcome the friction between the National Guard officers and troops, who formed the core of the unit, and the new influx of regular army officers and conscripts who had filled out the division for war.

In charge of the Engineer Special Brigades was **Brigadier General William Hoge**. His role in the training and planning of the vital engineer operations at Omaha Beach is often overlooked and he would win greater fame for his leadership of Combat Command B of the 9th Armored Division during the battle for St Vith during the Ardennes campaign.

The tactical command of forces landing on D-Day was in the hands of the regimental leaders. The 1st Division's 16th Infantry Regiment was led by **Lieutenant Colonel George Taylor**, an experienced veteran who had headed the regiment since the Tunisian campaign. The 29th Division's 116th Regiment was led by **Lieutenant Colonel Charles Canham**, a strict, by-the-book West Pointer nicknamed "Stoneface" by his troops. Although widely disliked by the enlisted men before D-Day, Canham's heroic performance on Omaha Beach abruptly changed opinions. He had a BAR shot from his hands and fought the rest of the day with one arm in an improvised sling, a .45cal pistol in his good hand. Canham's role has been overshadowed by the presence of the division's assistant commander, **Brigadier General Norman "Dutch" Cota**, who landed on the beach early in the day. Cota was the former chief of staff of the 1st Division and had fought in Tunisia. He was a charismatic combat commander, preferring to be in the field leading his troops rather than behind a desk.

Unlike most of the divisional and regimental commanders, the leader of the Ranger Provisional Group, **Lieutenant Colonel James E. Rudder**, was not a professional soldier. Rudder had graduated from Texas A&M in 1932 and was commissioned a second lieutenant in the Army reserves. He was a high school teacher until 1941, when he was called up to active duty and sent to the infantry school at Ft Benning. After further training at the Army Command and General Staff College in the autumn of 1942, he was posted to the 2nd Ranger Battalion, assuming command in the summer of 1943.

OPPOSING PLANS

THE AMERICAN PLAN

A good portrait shot of two GIs from the 1st Infantry Division onboard a Coast Guard LCI on the approaches to Normandy. The soldier in the foreground is wearing the assault jacket typical of the initial landings, and the Navy M-1926 inflatable life belt can be seen around his waist. (NARA)

O maha Beach was selected early in the Overlord planning since at the time it was undefended. On the negative side, the bluffs along the beach formed a significant tactical obstacle and were well suited for defense. Even after Rommel began fortifying the beach in the autumn of 1943, it remained an attractive option since it offered a deep-water anchorage only three-quarters of a mile from all parts of the beach with a full 36ft of water at low tide, making it an ideal location for an artificial harbor for follow-on operations. The terrain behind the beach was much more suitable for motor transport than at neighboring Utah Beach. In February 1944, First US Army conducted a study of Omaha Beach which concluded that, if defended by an infantry regiment, the configuration of the beach would multiply the combat power of the German troops and present a formidable defensive position assaulting which would likely result in heavy casualties. If it was defended by a full infantry division, it would be impregnable. The US Army, right up to the time of the landings, thought that the beach was only defended by a single, understrength, poor-quality regiment. As will be discussed further, this would prove to be the most significant mistake in the US plan. The German forces on Omaha Beach were more than three times those anticipated.

The most critical necessity in the Operation Neptune plan was the need for tactical surprise. Allied planners were very concerned that if the Germans suspected a landing in Normandy, they would reinforce the area to the point where an amphibious assault would be impossible. The need for surprise affected the bombardment of the battlefield in the weeks before the landing. Since the Allies did not want to tip their hand, this precluded any concentrated bombardment of the assault beaches by either sea or air. For every bomb dropped in the Normandy area, two or more were dropped in the Pas de Calais and Picardy areas

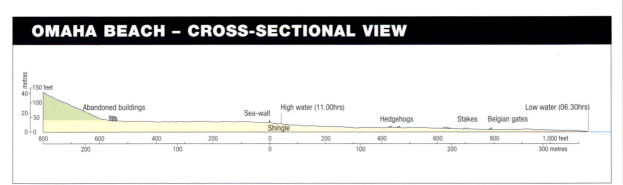

OMAHA BEACH – CROSS-SECTIONAL VIEW

The Omaha Beach Bombardment Group included ten destroyers. This is USS *Thompson* (DD-627) commanded by Lieutenant Commander A.L. Gebelin. She is seen here at the end of May 1944 being replenished at sea from the battleship USS *Arkansas* before setting off for Normandy. On D-Day the *Thompson* began by bombarding the Pointe-et-Raz-de-la-Percée and spent the afternoon providing fire support for the Rangers on Pointe-du-Hoc. (NARA)

to continue the Operation Fortitude ruse. The risk of this strategic choice paid off at all the beaches except Omaha.

Operation Neptune contemplated a dawn landing at low tide due to Rommel's new beach defenses, which placed anti-craft obstacles in the water close to shore. A dawn landing would make it less likely that the Germans would discover the invasion fleet during its movement to the beaches. The landings were scheduled to begin on 5 June 1944 but were postponed due to foul weather in the Channel. Eisenhower rescheduled the assault for Tuesday, 6 June 1944 after Allied meteorological services had discovered a break in the weather that would last for several days. By this time the enormous momentum of the operation also put pressure on Eisenhower to approve the attack, and his decision was reinforced by an intelligence report early in June from the Japanese ambassador in Berlin which indicated that Hitler was still convinced the attack would come on the Pas de Calais.

The amphibious assault was a carefully choreographed plan calling for a series of preliminary though short bombardments of the coast followed by amphibious landings. The initial naval element of Operation Neptune at Omaha Beach was Force O. The naval forces for the American beaches were originally named Forces X and Y, but to make them more comprehensible they were switched first to Omaha and Oklahoma, and then to their final names, Omaha and Utah, monikers that applied to the beaches as well. The bombardment ships consisted of two old battleships and three light cruisers, supported by 15 destroyers and numerous smaller ships and craft. The naval bombardment plan had three phases. At first light (0558hrs) the navy would begin the counter-battery phase, attacking all 14 known German artillery positions. Twenty minutes before the landings (H-20) the bombardment would shift to the attack of beach defenses, especially known fortifications. At H-hour, the fire would shift to targets behind the beachhead, or on the flanks. Admiral Hall was not happy with the "shoe-string naval force" allotted to

One innovation for the Normandy landings was the use of rocket craft. These LCT(R)(3) carry 1,080 5in. rockets. A total of 9,000 rockets were fired in the opening bombardment from nine LCT(R), but most accounts suggest their salvoes missed the beach. (NARA)

Task Force O and he wanted more destroyers. Due to tidal conditions, the landings would begin at Omaha Beach before other beaches and as a result the naval bombardment would be significantly shorter, only 40 minutes. Task Force O had neither the time nor the resources to fulfill its bombardment mission.

Shortly after the naval bombardment began, the US Army Air Force was scheduled to attack the defenses using heavy bombers. The bluff above the beach, the concrete emplacements in the draws, and the areas behind the beach were the primary targets. Contrary to what many Army troops believed, the plan did not call for attacks on the beach obstructions in order to avoid cratering the beach since this would make it difficult later in the day to move motorized transport off the beach. This attack would prove to be one of the most crucial failures at Omaha Beach on D-Day. The US Army Air Force liked to advertise its precision bombing capabilities, but in reality, the bomber commanders knew that there was still a considerable margin of error in their attacks, especially in poor weather. While collateral damage was of little concern when bombing German industrial targets, it was a significant concern when carrying out heavy strikes near US forces. The bombing mission required good weather for even modest precision and when the weather proved poor the Air Force changed the bombing tactics to limit any possible short-falls into the landing force. Due to the use of blind bombing using radar for targeting, the Air Force commanders ordered the bombardiers to delay their bomb release by 30 seconds once the coast was picked up on radar. This guaranteed that the bombs would fall far from the coastline. The lack of a contingency plan, such as the use of bombers under the cloud cover, was a major weakness of the plan, and the Army had unrealistic expectations of the air force's capabilities. There were no plans to use the Ninth Air Force in close-support missions against the beach defenses since the army lacked the communications to call in air strikes and no training had been undertaken.

Although the US Army Air Force conducted very effective air superiority and interdiction missions on D-Day, the US infantry widely blamed the air force for the lack of preparatory bombardment of Omaha Beach. This B-26C Marauder of the 450th Bombardment Squadron, 322nd Bomb Group is seen over the invasion fleet on D-Day. (NARA)

Since the Allies expected to confront fortifications along the beach, armored support was deemed essential. In theory, each regimental combat team (RCT) would be preceded onto the beach by three companies of tanks to knock out any remaining bunkers not destroyed by the bomber attack. After the Dieppe experience, the British army had developed an assortment of specialized tanks, dubbed "Funnies", to aid in amphibious assaults. The myth has developed over the years that the US Army spurned

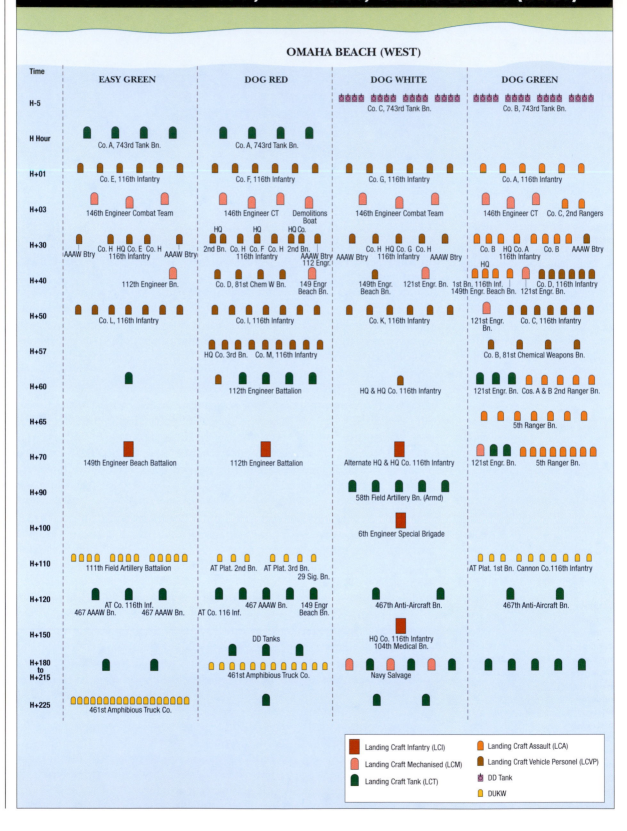

OMAHA BEACH (WEST)

Time	EASY GREEN	DOG RED	DOG WHITE	DOG GREEN
H-5			Co. C, 743rd Tank Bn.	Co. B, 743rd Tank Bn.
H Hour	Co. A, 743rd Tank Bn.	Co. A, 743rd Tank Bn.		
H+01	Co. E, 116th Infantry	Co. F, 116th Infantry	Co. G, 116th Infantry	Co. A, 116th Infantry
H+03	146th Engineer Combat Team	146th Engineer CT / Demolitions Boat	146th Engineer Combat Team	146th Engineer CT / Co. C, 2nd Rangers
H+30	AAAW Btry / Co. H HQ Co. E Co. H / 116th Infantry / AAAW Btry	HQ / 2nd Bn. Co. H Co. F / HQ / Co. H / HQ Co. / 2nd Bn. / 116th Infantry / AAAW Btry / 112 Engr.	AAAW Btry / Co. H HQ Co. G Co. H / 116th Infantry / AAAW Btry	Co. B HQ Co. A Co. B / 116th Infantry / AAAW Btry
H+40	112th Engineer Bn.	Co. D, 81st Chem W Bn. / 149 Engr Beach Bn.	149th Engr. Beach Bn. / 121st Engr. Bn.	HQ / 1st Bn. 116th Inf. / Co. D, 116th Infantry / 149th Engr. Beach Bn. / 121st Engr. Bn.
H+50	Co. L, 116th Infantry	Co. I, 116th Infantry	Co. K, 116th Infantry	121st Engr. Bn. / Co. C, 116th Infantry
H+57		HQ Co. 3rd Bn. / Co. M, 116th Infantry		Co. B, 81st Chemical Weapons Bn.
H+60		112th Engineer Battalion	HQ & HQ Co. 116th Infantry	121st Engr. Bn. / Cos. A & B 2nd Ranger Bn.
H+65				5th Ranger Bn.
H+70	149th Engineer Beach Battalion	112th Engineer Battalion	Alternate HQ & HQ Co. 116th Infantry	121st Engr. Bn. / 5th Ranger Bn.
H+90			58th Field Artillery Bn. (Armd)	
H+100			6th Engineer Special Brigade	
H+110	111th Field Artillery Battalion	AT Plat. 2nd Bn. AT Plat. 3rd Bn. / 29 Sig. Bn.		AT Plat. 1st Bn. Cannon Co.116th Infantry
H+120	AT Co. 116th Inf. / 467 AAAW Bn. 467 AAAW Bn. / 467 AAAW Bn.	AT Co. 116 Inf. / 467 AAAW Bn. / 149 Engr Beach Bn.	467th Anti-Aircraft Bn.	467th Anti-Aircraft Bn.
H+150		DD Tanks	HQ Co. 116th Infantry / 104th Medical Bn.	
H+180 to H+215		461st Amphibious Truck Co.	Navy Salvage	
H+225	461st Amphibious Truck Co.			

■ (red)	Landing Craft Infantry (LCI)	■ (orange)	Landing Craft Assault (LCA)
■ (pink)	Landing Craft Mechanised (LCM)	■ (brown)	Landing Craft Vehicle Personel (LCVP)
■ (green)	Landing Craft Tank (LCT)	■ (pink/DD)	DD Tank
		■ (yellow)	DUKW

The M4A1 Duplex Drive (DD) amphibious tanks consisted of a normal Sherman medium tank with a folding canvas buoyancy skirt and a modified propulsion system, derisively called "thirty tons of steel in a canvas bucket" by its crews. This DD is seen in Germany in 1945 during later river-crossing operations. (NARA)

the use of these specialized tanks. In fact, by February 1944, the US Army had submitted a request for 25 Sherman Crab anti-mine flail tanks, 100 Sherman Crocodile flamethrower tanks, and other Sherman combat engineer equipment for Overlord. The original US plans expected the use of the Churchill AVRE (Armoured Vehicle Royal Engineers) to support the engineer breaching operations. None of these were provided in time for D-Day as British industry could barely keep pace with the needs of the British Army. Since it would take time for US industry to manufacture these, priority was given to those items deemed most necessary – the controversial DD tanks. In place of the Churchill AVREs, V Corps was allotted 16 M4 dozer-tanks to assist the engineers.

The Duplex Drive (DD) tank was a cover name for an amphibious version of the Sherman medium tank, and was developed in Britain as a means to bring tanks ashore without the need for landing craft. The attraction of this scheme was that the tanks could be sent ashore in the first waves in a less conspicuous and less vulnerable fashion than by using

The alternative to DD tanks was to fit the M4 medium tank with wading trunks as had been the practice on Sicily and in the amphibious landings at Salerno and Anzio during the Italian campaign. One company in each of the two tank battalions landed on Omaha Beach had their tanks fitted with wading trunks, which protected the tanks engine from flooding and allowed the tank to crawl ashore with water up to the top of its turret. The tanks were further waterproofed by sealing gaps and openings to prevent the fighting compartment and engine compartment from leaking. (NARA)

large landing craft. Buoyancy was provided by a large canvas flotation screen around the tank, which folded like an accordion when not in use. The DD tank's canvas screen had only a foot of freeboard when in the water and anything like rough seas threatened to collapse or swamp the fragile screen. A pair of propellers were added at the rear of the hull that were powered off the tank's engine. Since British firms could not produce these in adequate numbers, conversion kits were built by Firestone in the US for M4A1 medium tanks. Of the 350 converted, about 80 tanks were transferred to British units to make up for shortages.

In past amphibious landings, such as Sicily and Salerno, the US Army had preferred to fit tanks with wading trunks, allowing them to be deposited by landing craft in shallow water beyond any beach obstructions and drive ashore. This also allowed the tanks to fire at beach targets during their run into the beach on the landing craft and remain in the surf, with their submerged hull protected by water, while engaging targets on the beach. The new DD tanks were greeted with skepticism by many US officers who doubted their seaworthiness. The V Corps commander, Gerow, opposed their use and would have preferred to land both tank battalions on Omaha with wading trunks. As a result of these misgivings, the US tank battalions slated for Operation Neptune were mixed formations equipped with two companies of DD tanks to land in the initial waves, and one company of tanks with wading trunks to land shortly afterward from LCTs. During pre-invasion exercises at Slapton Sands in Devon, Britain, a number of DD tanks sank, leading doubtful US Navy officials to insist on guidelines for launching them. An arrangement was reached under which the senior officer (army or navy) aboard the landing craft could make the judgment that the sea was too rough for the DD tanks to swim ashore and land them directly on the beach. The loophole in this procedure was that some of the young tank officers outranked the commanders of the landing craft but lacked the experience to evaluate the sea conditions.

One mystery has been why the US Army at Normandy did not use amtracs (amphibious tractors) to land troops as had been done in the Pacific theater since Tarawa in 1943. Bradley had brought back two of the best US divisional commanders from the Pacific to provide some seasoning to the European theater officers and one of these, J. Lawton Collins, was assigned as the corps commander at the neighboring Utah Beach. The other, Major General Charles Corlett, had landed with his 7th Division on Kwajalein in February 1944. Corlett arrived in the UK in April and was surprised to see that the landings would rely on LCVP and LCA landing craft instead of the amtracs now favored in the Pacific. He approached both Eisenhower and Bradley about the issue, but plans were so far along that his opinions were dismissed. The failure to consider the lessons of the Pacific campaign was mainly due to the conviction of the army in Europe that they had much more experience in large-scale amphibious landings than the army in the Pacific or the US Marines. There had been no landings in the Pacific on the scale of North Africa, Sicily, Salerno or Anzio and there would not be until after the Normandy landings. The amtracs had been used at Tarawa specifically to surmount the coral reef surrounding the atoll and this was not a feature of the Normandy beaches. What the US Army commanders in Europe failed to realize and their Pacific counterparts had come to recognize was that the amtracs were a necessity when landing on a contested, fortified beach. The amtracs could put the infantry ashore at the seawall, minimizing their exposure to small arms fire as they struggled from the landing craft, waded through the surf, and raced across hundreds of yards of beach. In fact, the US Army had shipped over 300 amtracs to Europe in 1944, but the lack of demand for their use in the Overlord plan meant that they were reserved for Operation Swordhilt, a contingency operation in which Patton's uncommitted Third Army was intended to reinforce Overlord in the event of a failure at one of the beaches.

American planning for Operation Neptune did not pay enough attention to a key difference between Normandy and previous landings in the Mediterranean, namely the fortified coast. None of the 1943 landings were contested on the shoreline and none involved landings against obstructed beaches. Normandy required tactics and equipment comparable to those for operations against fortifications. While considerable effort went into providing large numbers of engineers to tackle the fortifications at Normandy, neither the M4 tanks nor bulldozers were equipped to survive on a constricted beach targeted by numerous anti-tank guns. In February 1944 the US Army in Europe had requested an assault tank version of the M4A3 medium tank with sufficient armor to confront German bunkers on the Siegfried Line later in the European campaign. This emerged as the M4A3E2 assault tank, which could

A young GI from the 1st Infantry Division on the way to Normandy. He is wearing the distinctive assault jacket worn by the initial waves at Omaha Beach, and his M1 carbine is in plastic wrap to protect it from water. To the left is a pole charge for attacking pillboxes while to the right is an M1A1 bazooka. In front of him are pack charges and behind him bangalore torpedoes, all tied to inflated life belts to provide buoyancy in the water. (NARA)

A group from the 2nd Rangers enjoy Red Cross coffee and donuts in Weymouth, England, shortly before loading aboard their landing craft. They have their M5 assault gas-mask bags slung on their chests, a common practice on D-Day. (NARA)

withstand frontal hits from 88mm anti-tank guns, the largest gun encountered in Normandy. These might have made a difference on D-Day had there been more appreciation of the vulnerability of the existing M4 tank to contemporary German anti-tank guns. As it transpired the M4A3E2 did not arrive in Europe until the autumn but did prove very effective in the Siegfried Line campaign. The British already had an effective support tank in their thickly armored Churchill infantry tank and it was used with success on D-Day, including a specialized combat engineer version – the AVRE.

The other specialized forces landing in the first waves were the Gap Assault Teams, of which 16 were assigned to Omaha Beach. They were to blast gaps 50 yards wide through the beach obstructions to allow landing craft to continue to reach the beach once the tide began to rise. The plan gave these teams only about 30 minutes to carry out their tasks due to the rising tide. This was a vital mission since if the gaps were not cleared, the underwater obstacles would prevent follow-up landings by later waves of craft.

The main landings were to be conducted by two regimental combat teams (RCT) each consisting of an infantry regiment with attached engineers and other support troops. The left (eastern) flank would be assaulted by the 16th RCT based around the 16th Infantry Regiment, 1st Division, while the right (western) flank would be assaulted by the 116th RCT, based around the 116th Infantry, 29th Division. The engineers in the first wave were mainly from the divisional engineer battalions, but follow-on waves contained the 5th and 6th Provisional Engineer Brigades to assist in preparing the beach for follow-on forces and supplies. The tasks of the engineers included clearing the beach obstacles, for example using bangalore torpedoes to open gaps in wire obstructions, clearing lanes through minefields to provide the infantry with exits off the beach, and destroying German fortifications. After Dieppe the British army felt that combat engineers required armored support in the form of flail tanks to conduct minefield clearance, and specialized Churchill tanks with petard mortars for demolition work. The US Army ignored the use of armored engineer vehicles, except for armored bulldozers, due to a lack of experience in this type of operation.

The Ranger Provisional Brigade was assigned the most perilous mission of the assault – the capture of the German artillery battery on Pointe-du-Hoc on the western edge of the assault area. This heavily fortified battery could strike both Utah and Omaha Beach and Bradley deemed it essential that it be eliminated. Unfortunately, it was located on a promontory with cliffs all around. One officer remarked that an attacking force could be swept off the cliffs by "three old women with brooms." Pointe-du-Hoc was scheduled to receive special treatment from the naval bombardment force in advance of the Ranger attack but American commanders thought it was the single most difficult aspect of the attack on Omaha Beach.

After the first two regimental combat teams landed at dawn, additional reinforcements would arrive in successive waves bringing the total to four RCTs by midday. Force B would arrive in the afternoon, which would increase the strength on Omaha Beach to two reinforced divisions, with a third division to land on D+1.

Allied intelligence had detected the German 352nd Infantry Division around St Lô and anticipated that it would begin to move against the beachhead sometime on D-Day, and might reach the Aure River or even cross it on the afternoon of D-Day. However, the plan expected that it would delay, but not stop the advance to the D+1 positions.

THE GERMAN PLAN

The defenses along Omaha Beach increased continually after the autumn of 1943 when Rommel was put in charge of reinvigorating the Atlantic Wall. Although Hitler and most senior German commanders expected the main invasion to take place on the Pas de Calais, Rommel believed that a case could be made for landings on the Normandy coast, or in Brittany around Montagne d'Aree. As a result, he ordered the construction of defenses along the most likely areas of coastline and increased the forces ready to defend the coast. Defenses in Normandy were initially based around the 716th Infantry Division, a poor-quality, static division. Omaha Beach was patrolled by a single regiment of this division.

Rommel believed that the sea itself was the best defensive barrier and the terrain around Omaha Beach presented ample defensive opportunities. The initial defensive work began at the water's edge with the construction of obstructions against landing craft. The outer barrier, about 100 yards above the low-tide mark and 275yds from the seawall, consisted of a string of steel obstructions, called Cointet gates by the Germans and Belgian gates or Element C by the Allies. These were designed to block landing craft from approaching the beach. The next line of barriers about 30 yards closer to shore were wooden stakes that were planted in the sand facing seaward and buttressed like an enormous tripod. These stakes were usually surmounted by a Tellermine 42 anti-tank mine. These obstacles were designed to blow holes in the bottom of landing craft. In some sectors these were followed by *Hemmkurven*, called ramp obstacles by the Allies, which were a curved steel structure designed to obstruct the landing craft. Finally there was a row of "hedgehogs" of various types. The most common was the *Tschechenigel*, called "Rommel's Asparagus" by the Allies, which was an anti-craft/anti-tank obstruction made from steel beams. The obstructions on the tidal flats were primarily intended to prevent the approach of landing craft to the seawall during high tide. These were submerged and invisible at high tide, preventing landing craft crews from steering easily through any gaps. There were a total of 3,700 obstacles at Omaha Beach – the highest density of any of the D-Day beaches.

Some of the more unusual weapons deployed at Omaha Beach were the remote control "Goliath" demolition vehicles. These contained a high-explosive charge, and were intended to attack tanks or landing craft. However, they arrived only a day before the landings, and so were not used in combat. (NARA)

At the high-water mark was a swathe of shingle, round stones the size of golf balls, sometimes backed by a seawall. One or more rows of concertina wire or other barbed wire obstructions were placed immediately inland from this. Until the autumn of 1943 there were many small beach houses and other structures along the shoreline for vacationers and local residents. These were knocked down to deprive Allied infantry of cover. A few of the more substantial buildings along the shore were left intact, but were converted into infantry strongpoints. The beach area was heavily mined, though gaps that contained no mines were also marked with minefield warnings to confuse Allied troops.

In contrast to the other four Normandy beaches, which are relatively flat, Omaha Beach is characterized by bluffs rising up to 150ft from the sea, most noticeably on its western side. The edges of these bluffs provide ideal defensive positions for infantry with clear fields of fire on the exposed troops below. On some of the cliffs on the eastern side of

One of the more common defensive works in Normandy was this type of 50mm gun pit. The obsolete 50mm PaK 38 anti-tank gun was mounted on a new pintle for easier traverse and deployed within a concrete emplacement. There were three of these along Omaha Beach and many more inland, like this example on the approaches to Cherbourg. (NARA)

The most powerful weapons on Omaha Beach were two 88mm PaK 43/41 "Scheunentor" (barn door). These were located in casemates, but one was moved out of the bunker after the landings, as seen here. (NARA)

the beach, 240mm artillery shells were dangled over the cliff with trip-wires to serve as booby-traps for any infantry trying the climb. These were called "roller-grenades" and they were spaced some 330ft apart.

Access from the beach was limited to five gullies, called "draws" by the US Army, and only two of these were readily passable by armored vehicles or motor transport. These became the center point of German defenses at Omaha Beach. Since the tactical objective of the defense was to prevent the Allies from moving off the beach, all five draws were stiffly defended by establishing a fortified belt in and around them. Fourteen strongpoints (*wiederstandnester*), numbered WN60 through WN73, were created along the beach. Most of the draws were covered by a strongpoint on the hilltops on either side of the draw. Two other strongpoints were constructed on the Pointe-et-Raz-de-la-Percée promontory on the eastern side of the beach to provide enfilading fire along the beach, and the three other strongpoints were constructed immediately behind the beach, covering the exits from the draws.

The configuration of each of these strongpoints differed due to terrain, and they were still being built when the Allies landed on 6 June 1944. Generally they consisted of small pillboxes, or concrete reinforced "Tobruk" machine-gun pits, at the base of the bluff obstructing the entrances to the draws. The larger draws were also blocked by barrier walls, anti-tank ditches and anti-tank traps. One of the most effective defenses was the *Bauform 667* anti-tank gun bunkers built into the sides of the bluffs, with their guns pointed parallel to the beach. These

The artillery regiment of the 352nd Infantry Division was deployed in field emplacements about 6 miles behind the beach, like this 105mm leFH 18/40. Pre-sighted on targets along the beach, they proved to be one of the German defenders' most effective weapons on D-Day. (NARA)

bunkers had a defensive wall on the side facing the sea that made it very difficult for warships to engage them with gunfire. By careful positioning they prevented Allied tanks from entering the draw since they could hit the tanks on their vulnerable side armor from point-blank range and, furthermore, the guns were positioned to fire in defilade down the length of the beach. These often contained older anti-tank guns such as obsolete PaK38 50mm. However, such weapons were more than adequate to penetrate the side armor of the Sherman tank and they were also effective against landing craft. In total, there were eight anti-tank gun bunkers along Omaha Beach including two 88mm guns. Besides the fully enclosed anti-tank guns, there were three 50mm anti-tank guns on pedestal mounts in concrete pits, and ten other anti-tank guns and field guns in open pits in the various strongpoints. As an additional defensive installation, the turrets from obsolete French and German tanks were mounted over concrete bunkers. There were five of these on Omaha Beach, the heaviest concentration being in WN66/68 covering the D-3 Les Moulins draw. Generally the strongpoints had a mixture of these types of firing positions. For example, the WN61/62 strongpoint at the E-3 Colleville draw had two 75mm PaK 40 anti-tank guns in casemates to enfilade the beach, two 50mm anti-tank guns on pedestals in open concrete emplacements, a 50mm mortar Tobruk and six machine-gun Tobruks.

Around these fortifications, the German infantry dug out a series of trenches as a first step to creating a series of interlocking shelters and protected passages. However, the shortage of concrete in the spring of 1944 meant that only a small portion of these trench lines were concrete-reinforced. The construction of these defenses was hampered by the haphazard priorities of the army, Luftwaffe, and Organization

Normandy had lower priority than the Pas de Calais for concrete, so many of the German infantry positions were ordinary slit trenches like these from the WN66 strongpoint on the east shoulder of D-3 Les Moulins draw. (NARA)

Table 1: German Beach Strongpoints, Grandcamps Sector

Wiederstandnester	Location[2]	AT Gun Casemates	Panzerstellung	50mm AT gun pit	AT/Field guns	MG bunker/Tobruk	Mortar Tobruk
WN73	Near D-1	1					3
WN72	D-1	2				3	
WN71	D-1					3	1
WN70	D-1/D-3	1			1	4	2
WN68	D-3		2		1	1	
WN66	D-3		1	1	1	1	2
WN65	E-1	1		1	1		2
WN64	E-1				1		2
WN62	E-3	2			3		2
WN61	E-3	1	1	1		4	
WN60	F-1		1		2		3
Total		8	5	3	10	16	17

Todt. The Luftwaffe, for example, built an elaborate concrete shelter for its radar station on the neighboring Pointe-et-Raz-de-la-Percée that was absolutely useless in protecting the radar from any form of attack. At the same time many key infantry trenches on the bluffs, lacking concrete reinforcement, flooded during spring rain and were rendered useless by the time of the attack.

Of all the defenses near Omaha Beach, by far the most fortified was the Pointe-du-Hoc. The site was originally constructed to contain six 155mm guns in open gun emplacements, but the defense was being reconstructed to protect each gun with a fully enclosed *Bauform 671* ferro-concrete casemate. In addition, the site contained a fully enclosed artillery observation point on the seaward side of the promontory and fully protected crew shelters and ammunition bunkers.

Due to Rommel's tactical approach, most of the German tactical defenses were spread as a thin crust along the shoreline with very modest reserve forces behind the main line of resistance. On D-Day itself the tactical plan would simply be to hold the invading force on the beach with the resources at hand.

OPPOSING ARMIES

GERMAN FORCES

The 716th Infantry Division had garrisoned Omaha Beach, called the Grandcamps sector by the Germans, since June 1942. This under-strength, static division was spread from Carentan to the Orne estuary and, therefore, defending all of the Normandy beaches except Utah in the west. 726th Grenadier Regiment (GR.726) was responsible for covering the Omaha Beach area in 1942–43. Of the 58 divisions under OB West on 6 June 1944, 33 were static or reserve divisions. The troops in these static divisions tended to be older conscripts, typically about 35 years old. The fourth battalion of GR.726 was 439th Ost Battalion made up of former Red Army troops. The division was significantly under-strength with only about 7,000 troops compared to a nominal strength of over 12,000. On the other hand, most of its forces were deployed in bunkers or field fortifications with a large number of supplementary weapons including 197 machine-gun pits, 12 anti-tank rifles, 75 medium mortars, and 249 flamethrowers.

On 15 March 1944 the 352nd Infantry Division was ordered to take over defense of the Bayeux sector of the Normandy beaches as part of Rommel's effort to strengthen the defenses in this sector. This division had been formed in December 1943 near St Lô from the remnants of the battered 321st Infantry Division, which had been sent back from Russia to rebuild. The new division was organized as a Type 44 infantry division and most of its personnel were recent conscripts from the classes of 1925/26, meaning young men 18–19 years old. Unlike the old 716th Infantry Division, the 352nd Infantry Division was at full strength. It consisted of three infantry regiments, each with two rifle battalions with their companies numbered 1 through 4 and 5 through 8 respectively. The 13th Company was a cannon company for direct fire support equipped with two 150mm and six 75mm infantry howitzers. The 14th company in each regiment was an anti-tank unit with Panzerschreck anti-tank rocket launchers. The 1944 divisional structure substituted a fusilier regiment for the old reconnaissance battalion, with one company on bicycles and one company motorized. The division's artillery regiment had four battalions, three with 12 105mm howitzers each and the fourth with 12 150mm guns. The division's anti-tank battalion had a company with 14 PzJg 38(t) Ausf. M Marder III tank destroyers, another with ten StuG III assault guns, and a third with improvised 37mm guns on Opel trucks. Divisional training was hamstrung by the lack of fuel and ammunition as well as by the need to divert the troops to work on field fortifications to reinforce the Atlantic Wall. There was little opportunity for training above company level. This unit was reasonably well trained by German 1944 standards, though not by US Army standards. The 1944 German infantry division had less

A young German infantryman enjoys a cup of coffee while on the way to a POW camp in England after having been captured in Normandy. The troops of the 352nd Infantry Division were mostly 18–19-year-old conscripts with their tactical training cut short by the need to do construction work on beach defenses for the three months they were stationed along the Atlantic coast prior to D-Day. (NARA)

manpower than its US counterpart but more firepower, especially in automatic weapons.

The reconfiguration of the defenses along the Bayeux coast in late March 1944 more than tripled their strength. The Omaha Beach area that had been held by two battalions from GR.726 was now reinforced by two regiments of the 352nd Infantry Division along the coastline and a reinforced regiment as corps reserve within a few hours march of the coast. The two battalions of GR.726 in the Omaha Beach sector were subordinated to the headquarters of the 352nd Infantry Division and retained their mission of manning the coastal emplacements and trenches along the beach. 914th Grenadier Regiment (GR.914) was responsible for the Isigny/Pointe-du-Hoc sector west of Omaha Beach, while 916th Grenadier Regiment (GR.916) was responsible for the Omaha Beach sector as well as the eastern section of Gold Beach. The third regiment, 915th Grenadier Regiment (GR.915), and the division's 352nd Fusilier Battalion were formed into Kampfgruppe Meyer and stationed behind the coast near St Lô to serve as the corps reserve.

The reinforced 352nd Infantry Division was responsible for defending 33 miles of coastline, far beyond what was considered prudent in German tactical doctrine. This led to a number of arguments between Rommel and the divisional commander, GenLt Dietrich Kraiss. Rommel wanted all of the infantry companies deployed along the main line of resistance so they could fire on landing Allied troops. Kraiss wanted to adopt a more conventional defense with a relatively thin screen along the beach and most of the companies held in reserve behind the bluffs from where they could counter-attack any penetrations. In the end a compromise was reached. In the Omaha Beach sector one of its infantry battalions moved up to the coastline and deployed two of its companies in the forward defenses alongside GR.726, with the other companies in the villages a few miles from the beach. The other battalion formed a reserve for the regimental sector along with the division's self-propelled anti-tank battalion.

Omaha Beach was covered by 1st Battalion, 352nd Artillery Regiment (I/AR.352) headquartered at Etreham with three batteries of 105mm howitzers. This battalion had forward observation posts located in bunkers along the coast, significantly enhancing their lethality when employed against targets on Omaha Beach. 2nd Battalion, 352nd Artillery Regiment (II/AR.352), headquartered to the east at St Clement, also had Omaha Beach in range. The artillery battalions were provided with only one unit of fire, meaning 225 rounds per 105mm howitzer and 150 rounds for each 150mm gun. No resupply was available for a few days. The final element of the artillery in this sector was added on 9 May 1944 when a battery of heavy artillery rockets (*Nebelwerfer*) of Werfer-Regiment.84 was positioned in this sector. Behind the 352nd Infantry Division was the 1st Flak-Sturm Regiment of the Luftwaffe 11th Flak Division, adding 36 88mm guns to the defense of this sector.

Allied intelligence believed the entire 352nd Infantry Division was in corps reserve around St Lô when in fact only one of its three infantry regiments was in reserve on 6 June 1944. To explain its appearance in the fighting on Omaha Beach on D-Day the myth developed that the division had been deployed near the beach to conduct training a few days before D-Day. This was not the case and the division had been in place near Omaha Beach for more than two months before D-Day.

On the Pointe-du-Hoc promontory between Omaha and Utah beaches was the 2nd Battery of Army Coastal Artillery Regiment 1260 (2/HKAA.1260) equipped with six French 155mm guns and five light machine-guns. By June 1944 four of six casemates for the guns had been completed but heavy Allied bombing raids had reduced the ground around the batteries to a lunar landscape of craters. After the 25 April 1944 bombing, the battery had withdrawn its guns from the casemates to an orchard south of the point. In their place the crews had fabricated dummy guns from timbers that fooled Allied intelligence into thinking the guns were still present. At the time of the invasion the concrete emplacements around the forward observation bunker were reinforced by a company from GR.726.

Luftwaffe support for the beach defenses was nonexistent. On 4 June 1944 Luftflotte 3 had 183 day-fighters in northern France of which 160 were serviceable. There were few ground-attack aircraft due to the policy of hoarding these units on the Eastern Front. Allied air attacks on forward airfields were so intense that on 5 June 124 fighters were withdrawn from the coast to bases further inland and the supplies and support for these aircraft were not available until 6 or 7 June.

ORDER OF BATTLE: GERMAN FORCES, GRANDCAMPS SECTOR

352.Infanterie Division	Molay-Littry	**GenLt Dietrich Kraiss**
Grenadier Regiment.914	**Neuilly-la-Foret**	**Oberstleutnant Ernst Heyna**
I/GR.914	Osmanville	
II/GR.914	Catz	
Grenadier Regiment.915		
(detached to corps reserve)	**St Paul-du-Vernay**	**Oberstleutnant Karl Meyer**
I/GR.915	Juaye	
II/GR.915	Lantheuil	
Grenadier Regiment.916	**Trevieres**	**Oberstleutnant Ernst Goth**
I/GR.916	Ryes	
II/GR.916	Formigny	
Infanterie Regiment.726		
(from 716.Infanterie Div.)	**Sully**	**Oberstleutnant Walter Korfes**
I/IR.726	Maisons	
III/IR.726	Jucoville	
Ost-Battalion 439	Isigny	
Artillerie Regiment.352	**Molay-Littry**	**Oberstleutnant Karl Ocker**
I/AR.352	Etreham	
II/AR.352	St Clément	
III/AR.352	La Noë	
IV/AR.352	Asnieres-en-Bessin	
Fusilier Battalion.352		
(detached to corps reserve)	Caumont-l'Éventé	
Panzerjäger Battalion.352	Mestry	
Pioneer Battalion.352	St Martin-de-Blagny	

AMERICAN FORCES

The US plan for Omaha Beach began the attack with a single division that would expand to two divisions by the afternoon. Rather than land the two divisions in column, the left flank of the assault force was the 16th

Regimental Combat Team (RCT) from the 1st Infantry Division, while the right flank was the 116th RCT from the 29th Division, but subordinated for the initial phase of the operation to the 1st Infantry Division.

The 1st Infantry Division, named "Big Red One" after its shoulder patch, was the Army's most experienced division and had been personally selected for the landings by Bradley. The division had already fought in North Africa and on Sicily and was one of the few divisions in the UK with any combat experience. In view of its excellent performance in repulsing a German Panzer attack on the Gela beachhead on Sicily a year before, the 16th Infantry was a natural choice for the initial assault wave.

The 29th Division was nicknamed the "Blue and Gray" for its shoulder patch, symbolizing an amalgamation of the Union and Confederate traditions. This National Guard division was headquartered in Baltimore, Maryland, and as a mid-Atlantic border state between north and south, the division drew its units from Maryland and Virginia. As with nearly all National Guard divisions, the regular army insisted on filling out its senior command posts with professional officers as the National Guard had the reputation for granting ranks as political sinecures. It was also necessary to flesh out the division with conscripts. There was some friction in the unit between the Guardsmen, who were often neighbors with years of peacetime service together, and the new influx of regular army officers and conscripts. Gebhardt's strict training regimen in the UK before D-Day was intended to forge the division into a cohesive fighting force and the 29th Division proved to be one of the better National Guard divisions during the subsequent fighting in France.

Each regimental combat team was allotted a tank battalion for fire support, the 741st Tank Battalion in support of the 16th RCT and the 743rd Tank Battalion supporting the 116th RCT.

The task of eliminating the German artillery battery on Pointe-du-Hoc was assigned to the Provisional Ranger Group, consisting of the elite

2nd and 5th Ranger Battalions. Since the battery was located on a cliff top the battalion developed a number of unique solutions for quickly scaling the cliffs under fire. Ladders were fitted inside the cargo hold of DUKW amphibious trucks. These were difficult to operate unless located firmly against the base of the cliff, so the Rangers also developed a rocket-fired grapnel hook using standard 2in. rockets and portable projectors. The assault teams also carried climbing rope and light-weight ladders. The main assault would be conducted by the 225 men of Force A, with Cos. E and F, 2nd Rangers scaling the eastern side of Pointe-du-Hoc, and Co. D on the western side. Force B, based on Co. D, 2nd Rangers would scale the cliffs on the neighboring Pointe-et-Raz-de-la-Percée promontory to eliminate German positions there. Force C, consisting of the remainder of 2nd Rangers and the 5th Rangers, would remain offshore during the initial assault, reinforcing Force A if the mission proceeded according to plan, but landing with the 116th RCT if the mission failed in order to assault Pointe-du-Hoc from the land side. This mission was widely considered the most dangerous of any assignment on D-Day; the reason the Rangers were given the assignment.

The other key elements in the assault waves were the Gap Assault Teams of the Special Engineer Task Force. Each of these 16 teams was formed by combining a 13-man Naval Combat Demolition Unit (NCDU) with a 28-man army engineer unit. The latter were drawn from the two units supporting the assault wave, the 146th and 299th Engineer Combat Battalions. The task of each team was to blow a gap 50 yards wide in the beach obstructions to permit later waves of landing craft to pass through the obstacles when the tide rose. Each team was allotted a M4 tank-dozer that arrived separately on an LCT.

ORDER OF BATTLE: US FORCES, OMAHA BEACH

V Corps	**MajGen Leonard T. Gerow**
1st Infantry Division	MajGen Clarence R. Huebner
29th Infantry Division	MajGen Charles H. Gebhardt
Provisional Ranger Group	LtCol James Rudder
5th Engineer Special Brigade	Col William Bridges
6th Engineer Special Brigade	Col Paul Thompson

Force O
16th Regimental Combat Team

16th Infantry Regiment	Col George Taylor
741st Tank Battalion	
Special Engineer Task Force (b)	
7th Field Artillery Battalion	
62nd Armored Field Artillery Battalion	
197th AAA Battalion (AWSP)	
1st Engineer Battalion	
5th Engineer Special Brigade (-)	
20th Engineer Combat Battalion	
81st Chemical Weapons Battalion (motorized)	

116th Regimental Combat Team

116th Infantry Regiment	Col Charles Canham
2nd Ranger Battalion	
5th Ranger Battalion	
743rd Tank Battalion	
Special Engineer Task Force	
58th Armored Field Artillery Battalion	
111th Field Artillery Battalion	
6th Engineer Special Brigade (-)	
112th Engineer Combat Battalion	
121st Engineer Battalion	
81st Chemical Weapons Battalion	
467th Automatic Anti-Aircraft Weapons Battalion (SP)	
461st Amphibious Truck Company	

18th Regimental Combat Team

18th Infantry Regiment	Col George Smith Jr.
745th Tank Battalion	
32nd Field Artillery Battalion	
5th Field Artillery Battalion	
5th Engineer Special Brigade (-)	

Force B
115th Regimental Combat Team

115th Infantry Regiment	Col Eugene Slappey
110th Field Artillery Battalion	

175th Regimental Combat Team

175th Infantry Regiment	Col Paul Goode

26th Regimental Combat Team

26th Infantry Regiment	Col John Seitz
33rd Field Artillery Battalion	

D-DAY

The Initial Operations

D-Day was originally scheduled to begin on 5 June, but the appalling weather in the Channel forced a postponement until 6 June. The German meteorology service in the Atlantic had been rolled-up by determined Allied action in the preceding months and, as a result, most senior German commanders were convinced that any landing operations would be impossible for several days until the weather cleared. As a result, Rommel was in Germany and a number of senior commanders were away from their posts to conduct staff exercises. General Dollman had lowered the alert status of all of his troops, believing that the foul weather would preclude any Allied activity.

Around 2215hrs on 5 June the intelligence section of several German headquarters picked up a coded radio message to the French resistance indicating that the invasion would begin in the next 48 hours. Some reconnaissance aircraft were sent to sweep the Channel but many officers thought it was a false alarm. Seventh Army in Normandy was not alerted.

At 0030hrs Allied minesweepers began to clear paths through anticipated minefields, guided by markers placed on the beaches by midget submarines. In fact the Germans had not yet established any significant minefields off Omaha Beach. At 0300hrs Task Force O arrived 25,000yds off Omaha Beach and dropped anchor to prepare the landing craft. At 0330hrs the assault troops were called to their debarkation posts on the assault transports and loaded into the landing craft at 0415. The landing craft gradually set off from the assault transports over the next hour, aiming to arrive at the rendezvous point by 0600hrs. The sea was

LCVPs begin the move to shore on D-Day under the watchful eye of the USS *Augusta,* flagship of the Western Task Force. The landing craft had a 12-mile run to shore in seas with three- to four-foot waves. The navy censor has partly obscured the cruiser's radar masts in this photo. (NARA)

choppy with 3–4ft waves and an occasional interference wave[3] as high as 6ft. The wind was gusting from the northwest at 10–18 knots. As a result, more than half of the assault troops were seriously seasick even before the final approach to the beach.

Wehrmacht units were alerted at 0100hrs when 84th Corps headquarters first learned of paratroop drops in neighboring sectors of the 716th Infantry Division. Although Omaha Beach was not in the landing zone of the 82nd or 101st Airborne Divisions, the dispersion of the drop resulted in small numbers of paratroopers landing in the GR.914 positions west of Omaha Beach and near the artillery batteries of II/AR.352 behind the beach. Through the early morning hours reports flowed in of paratroop and glider landings in neighboring sectors. At 0310hrs General Marcks ordered the corps reserve, Kampfgruppe Meyer, to begin moving towards Montmartin-Deville in order to keep open the routes between the 709th Division at Utah Beach and the 352nd Division at Omaha. The decision to send the reserves after the paratroopers proved to be premature and a serious mistake. Later in the morning the force would be badly needed in the opposite direction. As a result, Kampfgruppe Meyer spent most of the morning marching westward, only to have their orders changed a few hours later and shifted in the opposite direction, all the while under air attack. The division's artillery positions began to come under air attack around 0320hrs, with especially heavy attacks on Pointe-du-Hoc around 0335. Darkness shrouded the Allied naval force and visibility was only about 10 miles, not enough to see the anchorage. The first reports of Allied naval vessels came from the right flank of the division positions at 0502hrs and by 0520 large numbers of Allied naval vessels had been spotted moving over the horizon.

---

3 An interference wave is an extra-high wave caused by the interaction of two opposing wave patterns.

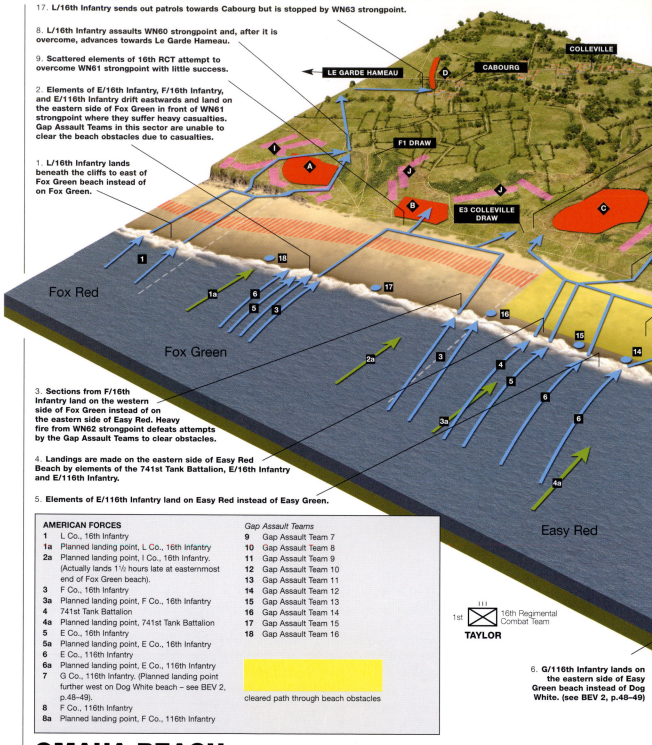

17. L/16th Infantry sends out patrols towards Cabourg but is stopped by WN63 strongpoint.

8. L/16th Infantry assaults WN60 strongpoint and, after it is overcome, advances towards Le Garde Hameau.

9. Scattered elements of 16th RCT attempt to overcome WN61 strongpoint with little success.

2. Elements of E/16th Infantry, F/16th Infantry, and E/116th Infantry drift eastwards and land on the eastern side of Fox Green in front of WN61 strongpoint where they suffer heavy casualties. Gap Assault Teams in this sector are unable to clear the beach obstacles due to casualties.

1. L/16th Infantry lands beneath the cliffs to east of Fox Green beach instead of on Fox Green.

3. Sections from F/16th Infantry land on the western side of Fox Green instead of on the eastern side of Easy Red. Heavy fire from WN62 strongpoint defeats attempts by the Gap Assault Teams to clear obstacles.

4. Landings are made on the eastern side of Easy Red Beach by elements of the 741st Tank Battalion, E/16th Infantry and E/116th Infantry.

5. Elements of E/116th Infantry land on Easy Red instead of Easy Green.

LE GARDE HAMEAU

CABOURG

COLLEVILLE

F1 DRAW

E3 COLLEVILLE DRAW

Fox Red

Fox Green

Easy Red

AMERICAN FORCES		Gap Assault Teams	
1	L Co., 16th Infantry	**9**	Gap Assault Team 7
1a	Planned landing point, L Co., 16th Infantry	**10**	Gap Assault Team 8
2a	Planned landing point, I Co., 16th Infantry. (Actually lands 1½ hours late at easternmost end of Fox Green beach).	**11**	Gap Assault Team 9
		12	Gap Assault Team 10
		13	Gap Assault Team 11
3	F Co., 16th Infantry	**14**	Gap Assault Team 12
3a	Planned landing point, F Co., 16th Infantry	**15**	Gap Assault Team 13
4	741st Tank Battalion	**16**	Gap Assault Team 14
4a	Planned landing point, 741st Tank Battalion	**17**	Gap Assault Team 15
5	E Co., 16th Infantry	**18**	Gap Assault Team 16
5a	Planned landing point, E Co., 16th Infantry		
6	E Co., 116th Infantry		
6a	Planned landing point, E Co., 116th Infantry		
7	G Co., 116th Infantry. (Planned landing point further west on Dog White beach – see BEV 2, p.48–49)		
8	F Co., 116th Infantry		
8a	Planned landing point, F Co., 116th Infantry		

cleared path through beach obstacles

1st ⊠ 16th Regimental Combat Team

TAYLOR

6. G/116th Infantry lands on the eastern side of Easy Green beach instead of Dog White. (see BEV 2, p.48–49)

OMAHA BEACH
16TH REGIMENTAL COMBAT TEAM SECTOR

6 June 1944, 0630hrs onwards, viewed from the northwest showing 16th RCT's landings on "Fox" and "Easy" beaches, the eastern sector of Omaha Beach. The first wave suffers heavy casualties but with the arrival of the second wave US troops begin to climb the bluffs and overcome the German defenses.

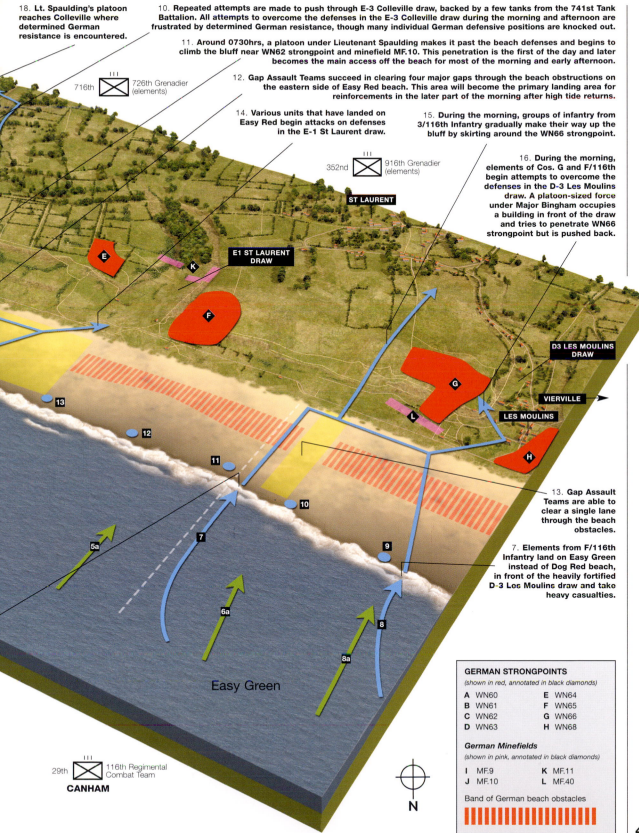

18. Lt. Spaulding's platoon reaches Colleville where determined German resistance is encountered.

10. Repeated attempts are made to push through E-3 Colleville draw, backed by a few tanks from the 741st Tank Battalion. All attempts to overcome the defenses in the E-3 Colleville draw during the morning and afternoon are frustrated by determined German resistance, though many individual German defensive positions are knocked out.

11. Around 0730hrs, a platoon under Lieutenant Spaulding makes it past the beach defenses and begins to climb the bluff near WN62 strongpoint and minefield MF.10. This penetration is the first of the day and later becomes the main access off the beach for most of the morning and early afternoon.

12. Gap Assault Teams succeed in clearing four major gaps through the beach obstructions on the eastern side of Easy Red beach. This area will become the primary landing area for reinforcements in the later part of the morning after high tide returns.

14. Various units that have landed on Easy Red begin attacks on defenses in the E-1 St Laurent draw.

15. During the morning, groups of infantry from 3/116th Infantry gradually make their way up the bluff by skirting around the WN66 strongpoint.

16. During the morning, elements of Cos. G and F/116th begin attempts to overcome the defenses in the D-3 Les Moulins draw. A platoon-sized force under Major Bingham occupies a building in front of the draw and tries to penetrate WN66 strongpoint but is pushed back.

716th | 726th Grenadier (elements)

352nd | 916th Grenadier (elements)

ST LAURENT

E1 ST LAURENT DRAW

E

K

F

D3 LES MOULINS DRAW

G

VIERVILLE →

L

LES MOULINS

H

13. Gap Assault Teams are able to clear a single lane through the beach obstacles.

7. Elements from F/116th Infantry land on Easy Green instead of Dog Red beach, in front of the heavily fortified D-3 Les Moulins draw and take heavy casualties.

13

12

11

5a

7

10

6a

9

8

8a

Easy Green

29th | 116th Regimental Combat Team

CANHAM

N

GERMAN STRONGPOINTS
(shown in red, annotated in black diamonds)

A	WN60	E	WN64
B	WN61	F	WN65
C	WN62	G	WN66
D	WN63	H	WN68

German Minefields
(shown in pink, annotated in black diamonds)

| I | MF.9 | K | MF.11 |
| J | MF.10 | L | MF.40 |

Band of German beach obstacles

45

Task Force O began to approach Omaha Beach and the battleships and destroyers began the preliminary naval bombardment at 0545hrs, lasting until 0625. Many inland German positions reported these as air attacks. The initial targets were behind the beach and at dawn the warships shifted their sights to specific targets along the beach. Aerial bombardment of positions behind the beach was scheduled to begin at 0600hrs but the decision to delay bomb release for 30 seconds after passing over the coast meant that none of the bombs fell on their intended targets. Most exploded harmlessly in the pastures south of the landing beaches. Of the 446 B-24 bombers taking part, 329 dropped 13,000 bombs. At 0610hrs five LCG(L) monitors approached the beach and added their gunfire to the naval bombardment. A few moments before H-hour nine LCT(R)s approached the beach and fired 9,000 rockets. These were a major disappointment due to their poor accuracy, and none were seen to hit the beach.

THE FIRST ASSAULT WAVE, 0530–0700HRS

The four companies of DD tanks were supposed to be launched from LCT6s around 0530hrs to give them time to swim the 5,000 yards to shore by H-Hour – 0630hrs. The naval officer in charge of the eight craft carrying the DD tanks of the 743rd Tank Battalion was convinced that the water was too rough for the tanks to swim ashore and reached agreement with the tank commander to land the tanks directly onto the beach. The LCTs landed the DD tanks on Dog Green and Dog Red beaches starting at 0629hrs. Company B, coming into the beach at the Vierville draw (Exit D-1), came under heavy anti-tank gunfire. The LCT carrying the company commander was sunk immediately offshore and four other tanks from the company were disabled before reaching the beach. Machine-gun fire from the German pillboxes damaged several other LCTs but all withdrew safely. Company A with the normal M4 tanks with wading trunks landed about the same time, so that 40 out of 48 tanks made it to shore.

An LCVP from the USS *Samuel Chase* with Coxswain D. Nivens at the helm was raked by German machine-gun fire as it approached the beach, which detonated explosives being carried by the infantry and started a fire. The craft safely landed and later returned to the transport. (NARA)

The final approach to the beach by LCVPs carrying the 16th RCT from the USS *Samuel Chase* during the second wave on D-Day around 0730hrs. The troops on the craft ahead have already disembarked and are wading to shore. (NARA)

To the west the situation was much worse. The two captains from the 741st Tank Battalion outranked the senior naval officers and insisted that the DD tanks be launched as ordered 5,000 yards offshore at 0540hrs. The DD tanks immediately encountered problems on entering the water, a few sinking immediately when their fragile canvas screens collapsed. They valiantly tried to swim ashore, but the combination of wind and sea conditions and tidal currents sank all but two tanks from Co. B. Of the tank crews, 33 drowned while the rest were rescued by accompanying vessels. Having watched the first of the four DD tanks on his craft sink immediately after leaving the ramp, the young skipper of LCT-600 decided to drop the remaining three on the beach. As a result, of the 32 DD tanks of the 741st Tank Battalion only five made it to shore on Easy Red beach. Following the two doomed companies of DD tanks was Co. A with M4A1 tanks with wading trunks; each LCT carrying two regular tanks and a dozer-tank. The luckless 741st lost two M4s and an M4 dozer-tank when their LCT struck a mine and sank. As a result, only

The deadliest sector of Omaha Beach for the initial wave was at the western end, Charlie and Dog Green beaches. This aerial view taken in 1945 shows how the German strongpoints on the cliffs of Pointe-et-Raz-de-la-Percée (to the right) could cover the beach with enfilading fire. At the very top of the picture is the D-1 Vierville draw. (MHI)

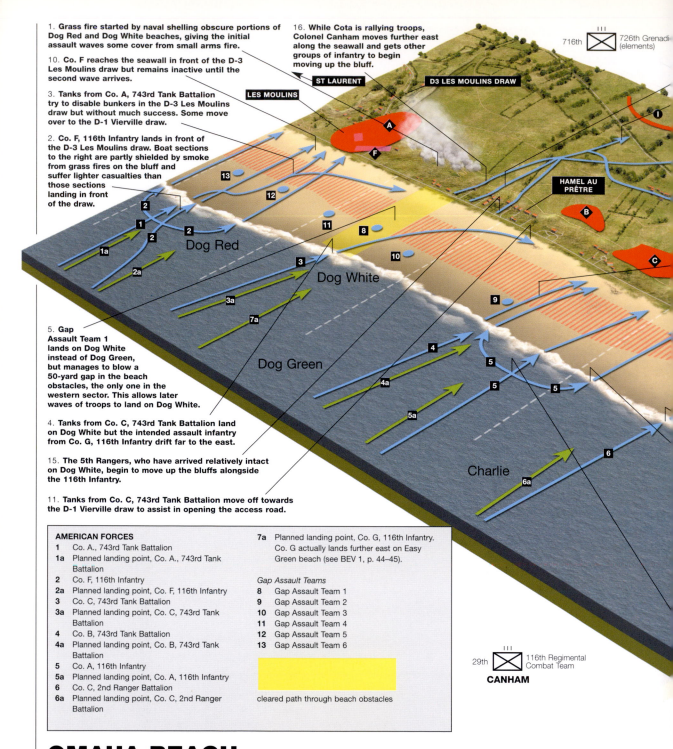

1. Grass fire started by naval shelling obscure portions of Dog Red and Dog White beaches, giving the initial assault waves some cover from small arms fire.

10. Co. F reaches the seawall in front of the D-3 Les Moulins draw but remains inactive until the second wave arrives.

3. Tanks from Co. A, 743rd Tank Battalion try to disable bunkers in the D-3 Les Moulins draw but without much success. Some move over to the D-1 Vierville draw.

2. Co. F, 116th Infantry lands in front of the D-3 Les Moulins draw. Boat sections to the right are partly shielded by smoke from grass fires on the bluff and suffer lighter casualties than those sections landing in front of the draw.

5. Gap Assault Team 1 lands on Dog White instead of Dog Green, but manages to blow a 50-yard gap in the beach obstacles, the only one in the western sector. This allows later waves of troops to land on Dog White.

4. Tanks from Co. C, 743rd Tank Battalion land on Dog White but the intended assault infantry from Co. G, 116th Infantry drift far to the east.

15. The 5th Rangers, who have arrived relatively intact on Dog White, begin to move up the bluffs alongside the 116th Infantry.

11. Tanks from Co. C, 743rd Tank Battalion move off towards the D-1 Vierville draw to assist in opening the access road.

16. While Cota is rallying troops, Colonel Canham moves further east along the seawall and gets other groups of infantry to begin moving up the bluff.

ST LAURENT

LES MOULINS

D3 LES MOULINS DRAW

HAMEL AU PRÊTRE

716th ⊠ 726th Grenadier (elements)

Dog Red

Dog White

Dog Green

Charlie

29th ⊠ 116th Regimental Combat Team

CANHAM

AMERICAN FORCES

1   Co. A., 743rd Tank Battalion
1a   Planned landing point, Co. A., 743rd Tank Battalion
2   Co. F, 116th Infantry
2a   Planned landing point, Co. F, 116th Infantry
3   Co. C, 743rd Tank Battalion
3a   Planned landing point, Co. C, 743rd Tank Battalion
4   Co. B, 743rd Tank Battalion
4a   Planned landing point, Co. B, 743rd Tank Battalion
5   Co. A, 116th Infantry
5a   Planned landing point, Co. A, 116th Infantry
6   Co. C, 2nd Ranger Battalion
6a   Planned landing point, Co. C, 2nd Ranger Battalion

7a   Planned landing point, Co. G, 116th Infantry. Co. G actually lands further east on Easy Green beach (see BEV 1, p. 44–45).

Gap Assault Teams
8   Gap Assault Team 1
9   Gap Assault Team 2
10   Gap Assault Team 3
11   Gap Assault Team 4
12   Gap Assault Team 5
13   Gap Assault Team 6

cleared path through beach obstacles

OMAHA BEACH
116TH REGIMENTAL COMBAT TEAM SECTOR

6 June 1944, 0629hrs onwards, viewed from the northwest showing 116th RCT's landings on "Dog" and "Charlie" beaches, the western sector of Omaha Beach. As in the eastern sector, the troops in the first assault wave suffer heavily. However, the efforts of General Norman "Dutch" Cota and Lieutenant Colonel Charles Canham help restore momentum to the US troops and they begin to press inland.

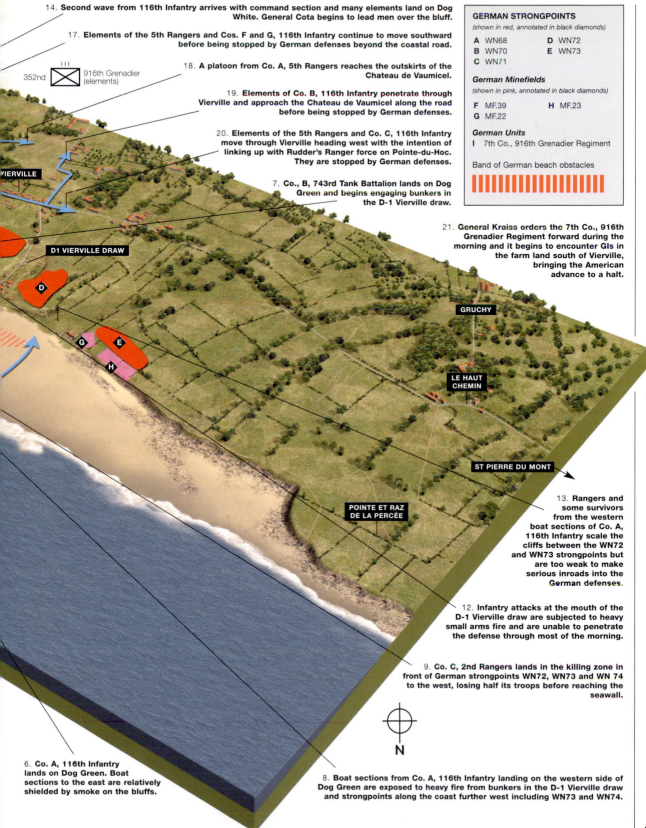

14. Second wave from 116th Infantry arrives with command section and many elements land on Dog White. General Cota begins to lead men over the bluff.

17. Elements of the 5th Rangers and Cos. F and G, 116th Infantry continue to move southward before being stopped by German defenses beyond the coastal road.

18. A platoon from Co. A, 5th Rangers reaches the outskirts of the Chateau de Vaumicel.

19. Elements of Co. B, 116th Infantry penetrate through Vierville and approach the Chateau de Vaumicel along the road before being stopped by German defenses.

20. Elements of the 5th Rangers and Co. C, 116th Infantry move through Vierville heading west with the intention of linking up with Rudder's Ranger force on Pointe-du-Hoc. They are stopped by German defenses.

7. Co., B, 743rd Tank Battalion lands on Dog Green and begins engaging bunkers in the D-1 Vierville draw.

21. General Kraiss orders the 7th Co., 916th Grenadier Regiment forward during the morning and it begins to encounter GIs in the farm land south of Vierville, bringing the American advance to a halt.

352nd | 916th Grenadier (elements)

GERMAN STRONGPOINTS
(shown in red, annotated in black diamonds)

A WN68	D WN72
B WN70	E WN73
C WN71	

German Minefields
(shown in pink, annotated in black diamonds)

| F MF.39 | H MF.23 |
| G MF.22 | |

German Units

I 7th Co., 916th Grenadier Regiment

Band of German beach obstacles

VIERVILLE

D1 VIERVILLE DRAW

GRUCHY

LE HAUT CHEMIN

ST PIERRE DU MONT

POINTE ET RAZ DE LA PERCÉE

13. Rangers and some survivors from the western boat sections of Co. A, 116th Infantry scale the cliffs between the WN72 and WN73 strongpoints but are too weak to make serious inroads into the German defenses.

12. Infantry attacks at the mouth of the D-1 Vierville draw are subjected to heavy small arms fire and are unable to penetrate the defense through most of the morning.

9. Co. C, 2nd Rangers lands in the killing zone in front of German strongpoints WN72, WN73 and WN 74 to the west, losing half its troops before reaching the seawall.

6. Co. A, 116th Infantry lands on Dog Green. Boat sections to the east are relatively shielded by smoke on the bluffs.

8. Boat sections from Co. A, 116th Infantry landing on the western side of Dog Green are exposed to heavy fire from bunkers in the D-1 Vierville draw and strongpoints along the coast further west including WN73 and WN74.

N

18 of its 48 tanks reached shore and three were knocked out by anti-tank guns almost immediately. In spite of their losses, the tanks attempted to carry out their mission and began engaging the various bunkers and defensive works.

The first assault wave, consisting of 1,450 men in eight infantry companies and the Gap Assault Teams, began landings at 0631hrs. Each LCVP or LCA usually carried 31 men and an officer, with six landing craft to a company. Few of the LCVPs made dry landings, with most grounding on sandbars 50–100 yards out. As the ramps dropped, the landing craft were subjected to a fusillade of machine-guns and gunfire. Some GIs had to wade through neck-deep water under savage fire the entire way. The troops in the assault wave had been issued much more equipment than normal infantry, including explosive charges and additional supplies, which made the passage through the surf especially difficult. Exhausted and sea-sick, when the survivors reached the water's edge there was little refuge. The expected bomb craters were nowhere to be seen and it was a 200-yard dash to the only reliable cover – the shingle and seawall. Many troops simply collapsed, or tried to find cover behind the numerous beach obstructions.

The conditions varied from sector to sector. Company G, 116th RCT landing west of the D-3 Les Moulins draw faced far less gunfire than on other beaches as grass fires started by the naval bombardment helped obscure the landing area. Company F, landing immediately in front of the D-3 Les Moulins draw were partly shielded by the smoke, but the three sections furthest east were exposed and suffered 50 per cent casualties by the time they reached the cover of the shingle. Company A, 116th RCT and Co. C, 2nd Rangers, landing furthest west on Dog Green opposite the D-1 Vierville draw, were slaughtered by the most intense fire encountered in any landing area in the 116th RCT sector. Not only was there a concentration of fortifications in the draw itself but there was enfilading fire from the WN72 and WN73 strongpoints on the

Pointe-et-Raz-de-la-Percée promontory on their right flank. The first Co. A landing craft grounded about 1,000yds from shore in deep water and few men made it to the beach. One LCA was hit by four mortar rounds in rapid succession and disintegrated. Every single soldier in the company commander's LCA was killed. Within moments most of the company's officers and NCOs were dead or wounded and two-thirds of Co. A, 116th Infantry were casualties. The 1/116th Infantry lost three of its four company commanders and 16 junior officers before even reaching the shoreline. Leaderless and under intense fire, the survivors clung to any protection available, mainly the beach obstacles. The company from the 2nd Rangers lost 35 of their 64 men before reaching the base of a cliff at the eastern edge of the beach. (The slaughter depicted in the opening sequence of the film *Saving Private Ryan* depicts this beach.)

On the beaches to the east assaulted by the 16th RCT the situation was bloody chaos. Problems with the control craft and the strong current caused many landing craft to drift eastward and many units landed far from their objectives. The landings on Easy Red between the St Laurent and Colleville draws were the most weakly defended and two sections of Co. E, 16th RCT made it to the shingle with modest losses but with few items of heavy equipment, which were abandoned while swimming ashore. A section from Co. F landing further east came under heavy fire when disembarking from their LCVP in neck-deep water and only 14 men reached the shore. The fire was much more intense on Fox Green beach to the east where Co. F, 16th RCT put ashore, opposite the heavily defended E-3 Colleville draw. Most of the casualties occurred after the ramps were dropped when machine-gun fire from the bunkers cut a swathe through the disembarking troops. On one LCVP only seven of the original 32 GIs reached the beach. Within moments Co. F had lost six officers and half its troops. Company E, 116th RCT had the misfortune of being further from their assigned beach than any other, and landed on Fox Green. They lost a third of their men, including the company commander, before reaching the shingle.

The two other companies of the 16th RCT were also scheduled to land on Fox Green, but Co. L wandered too far east and arrived 30 minutes late at the eastern extreme of Fox Green. Although suffering 35 per cent casualties, it was the only company of the first assault wave to remain a coherent unit. Company I became even more disoriented and drifted much too far east before their navigation was corrected. They landed $1\frac{1}{2}$ hours late in front of the cliffs at the easternmost edge of Fox Green.

The heavy losses amongst the infantry were also suffered by the critical Gap Assault Teams. Team 11 landed in front of the E-1 St Laurent draw and, while dragging ashore their rubber boat loaded with explosives, artillery hit the demolition charges, obliterating the team. Team 15 near the E-3 Colleville draw suffered the same fate and an artillery round struck the explosives of the neighboring Team 14 while still aboard the LCM, killing the entire navy contingent. Team 12 managed to plant their explosives on the obstacles on Easy Red beach but hesitated to detonate them due to the many wounded infantrymen near them. A mortar round hit some primacord, setting off the charges and killing or wounding most of the team and many of the nearby infantry. Team 13 was working on obstacles when German fire set off some of the charges, killing the Navy

section of the team. Team 7 was ready to breach a set of obstacles when an LCM crashed into the outer barrier, setting off seven Teller mines. Although these teams were supposed to be supported by M4 dozer-tanks, only six of the 16 made it ashore safely and three of these were quickly knocked out. By the end of the day only one dozer-tank was still operational. In spite of the heavy losses in front of the E-3 Colleville draw, several gap teams landed further east than planned due to the tides and so helped blow four adjacent gaps along the beach between the E-1 and E-3 exits. This accomplishment would prove crucial later in the day, since this was the only gap wide enough to accommodate a large number of landing craft.

The first infiltrations through the German defenses were made here around 0720hrs. Courage is not the absence of fear, but the ability to act in spite of fear. In the face of intense small arms, mortar and artillery fire, a handful of young soldiers began to act. Many young squad and platoon leaders tried to rally their men, but most were cut down by intense small arms fire. After engineers breached some wire obstructions, Sergeant Philip Streczyk from Co. E, 16th RCT ran through a gap at the base of the bluff west of the E-3 Colleville draw. Under covering fire from Co. G, Lieutenant John Spalding rallied a platoon-sized force and followed. Spalding's small force began to attack strongpoint WN62 from behind. In the meantime, the battered Co. F, 16th RCT had begun to attack the WN62 pillboxes from the front, putting one out of action with a bazooka. There were also penetrations into the F-1 draw by scattered groups of GIs who attacked the WN61 strongpoint from both front and rear. At 0720hrs a M4A1 tank of the battered 741st Tank Battalion managed to knock out the 88mm gun casemate at WN61. Around 0745hrs another M4A1 knocked out the top casemate at WN62 on the west side of the E-3 Colleville draw. The commander of GR.726 in this sector radioed back to 352nd Infantry Division headquarters that his telephone lines had been disrupted by the

A machine-gun team from Co. L, 16th Infantry moves under the protective cover of the cliffs on the eastern side of Omaha Beach during the initial effort to push through the F-1 draw and capture the WN60 strongpoint. (NARA)

attack and asked for a counter-attack to throw back the American penetration. The divisional commander, General Kraiss, radioed to the 84th Corps HQ since his GR.915 was in corps reserve as Kampfgruppe Meyer. At 0735hrs the request for a counter-attack was granted and at 0750 Kampfgruppe Meyer began dispatching a battalion towards Colleville that was scheduled to arrive around 0930. It was so far west chasing paratroopers that it didn't arrive until the afternoon. While it was not apparent at the time, the German defenses had already begun to crumble.

The gap teams were far less successful in the 116th RCT sector, in part due to the eastward drift of some landing craft. Team 1 inadvertently missed the killing zone on Dog Green, landing on Dog White instead. They blew a 50-yard gap in textbook fashion in only 20 minutes. The neighboring Teams 2 to 5 had little or no success. Team 2 arrived too late, while Team 3 suffered a direct artillery hit on its LCT and only one of the 40-man team survived. Team 4 suffered heavy casualties in front of the D-3 Les Moulins draw. Team 5 managed to plant its charges, but by the time it was ready to detonate them, so many infantry had huddled around the obstacles for shelter that only a few could be blown. Team 6 landed east of the D-3 Les Moulins draw and managed to create a gap in spite of the infantry using the obstacles for cover. Teams 7 and 8 had an impossible time clearing the obstructions, in part due to casualties and in part due to the recurring problem of the infantry using the obstacles as cover from the deadly German small arms fire. The two narrow gaps in the 116th RCT sector, while not as wide as the gaps to the east, would become the only means for reinforcement during much of the morning. Casualties among the Gap Assault Teams in both sectors were 41 per cent and some of the teams were virtually wiped out.

By 0700hrs the tide had turned and the obstacle belt was slowly inundated, drowning the badly wounded who had taken shelter near the beach obstructions. The surviving members of the eight infantry and one Ranger companies hid behind the shingle and seawalls along 7,000 yards of beach, losing more and more men as German mortar and machine-gun fire took their toll. Many of the GIs had a difficult time engaging the German positions as their rifles had become fouled with seawater or sand. Of the troops who landed in the first wave, more than a third were casualties within the first hour and most units were leaderless, their officers and NCOs dead or wounded.

THE SECOND ASSAULT WAVE, 0700–0800HRS

The second assault wave was supposed to land at 0700 in the midst of an advancing tide. The second wave had as many navigation problems as the first, exacerbated by the remaining, partly submerged obstacles. Company B, 116th RCT landing on Dog Green took heavy casualties like the first wave. Company C landed on Dog White enjoying the cover provided by the grass fires. Company D lost several LCVPs on the way into the beach and landed in a disorganized fashion with heavy casualties. The headquarters company landed at the extreme western area of the beach near the foot of the cliffs and was pinned down by sniper fire for most of the day. Company H and the 2/116th Infantry headquarters company landed on either side of the D-3 Les Moulins draw. Casualties amongst the officers of 2/116th Infantry was particularly heavy with two of the company commanders dead and another wounded. While the second wave landed, the tanks tried to reduce the German strongpoints. Three M4 tanks from the 743rd Tank Battalion began to crawl up the bluff near WN70, while three more began an assault on WN68 on the western side of the D-3 Les Moulins draw, penetrating the first layer of the defense.

The 3/116th RCT was scheduled to follow around 0730hrs. Aside from Cos. A and B, 2nd Rangers which landed in the killing zone near Dog Green, most of the later infantry companies and the 5th Rangers made it to shore with fewer casualties than the preceding waves and

GIs look warily towards the beach during landings on Omaha later on D-Day morning. The beach is already littered with vehicles and tanks knocked out earlier in the day. (NARA)

were soon crowding the beaches on either side of the D-3 Les Moulins draw. Around 0730hrs the regimental command parties began arriving including Col Canham and BrigGen Cota. Two LCIs bringing in the alternate HQ for 116th RCT were hit by artillery fire around 0740hrs and they burned for the rest of the day. To further add to the confusion on the beach, the second wave landings also brought to shore an increasing number of vehicles, which became bunched up along the shoreline and easy targets for German gunners. By 0800hrs the tide had risen by 8ft, covering many obstacles and drowning many of the severely wounded.

Cota and Canham walked along the beach, cajoling the men to move towards the bluffs above. After making a breach in the concertina wire beyond the seawall, around 0750hrs Cota led forward a small group of men from Co. C, 116th Infantry. They waded through tall reeds and marsh grass at the base of the bluffs, finally finding their way up onto the bluffs themselves using the terrain to avoid the German machine-gun positions. Ragged columns of troops followed, some being hit by sniper fire or wandering onto mines. Further east along Dog Red beach, Col Canham led a similar column from Cos. F and G, 116th Infantry

An Air Force reconnaissance aircraft provides a bird's-eye view of Omaha Beach on D-Day. In the center is an LCI(L) while to either side are LCTs. There is a string of DUKW amphibious trucks moving in column ashore. (NARA)

over the bluffs. Around 0810hrs the neighboring 5th Ranger Battalion blew four gaps in the wire. They made their way to the top of the bluffs by 0900hrs, parallel to Cota's and Canham's growing bands. As the groups reached the crest of the bluff, they began to coalesce and send out patrols. A small group of Rangers under Lieutenant Charles Parker set off for Château de Vaumicel to carry out their mission at Pointe-du-Hoc. Sometime after 1000hrs, once enough troops had finally gathered, Cota ordered Co. C, 116th Infantry and a platoon from 5th Rangers into the village of Vierville while other elements of the 5th Rangers moved to the southwest to cut the roads leading out of Vierville.

The first attempt to climb the bluffs east of the D-3 Les Moulins draw failed. Major Sidney Bingham, the 2nd Battalion commander, whose own companies had been decimated by the bunkers in the Les Moulins draw, tried rallying the leaderless men of Co. F who had landed in the first wave. He led them in the capture of a house in the mouth of the D-3 Les Moulins draw and then attempted to attack the WN66 strongpoint on the eastern shoulder of the draw. However, the German defensive positions were too strong and the GIs had to retreat to the protection of the house and neighboring trenches. A number of squads from Co. G had more success on the bluffs east of Les Moulins draw by skirting behind the WN66 strongpoint. When the 3/116th RCT landed relatively unscathed in this area, it provided the momentum to finally push inland and by 0900hrs there were portions of three companies over the bluffs between the D-3 and E-1 draws. By late morning there were about 600 GIs over the bluffs advancing southward. The scattered tanks fought a day-long battle

LANDINGS AT EASY RED BEACH, 0730HRS (pages 56–57)
This boat section of assault troops from 1st Battalion, 16th Infantry huddle inside their LCVP as it approaches Easy Red beach around 0730hrs during the second wave of landings. The tide has already started to turn, and some of the beach obstructions (1) are already awash. A M4A1 medium tank (2) with the number 10 on its wading trunk can be seen in the water to the left. The intended tactic for these tanks was to remain in the water with only the turret exposed, thereby protecting the hull from German anti-tank gun fire. In the event, most tanks drove onto the beach. Each LCVP carried one officer and 31 enlisted men. The standard loading pattern in the craft were three men abreast in 11 rows. The first two rows were the boat team leader, in this case a young lieutenant (3), and rifle team armed with M1 Garand rifles. They were followed by a four-man wire-cutting team, two BAR automatic weapons teams, a four-man 60mm mortar team, two two-man bazooka teams, a two-man flamethrower team, a five-man demolition team, and the assistant boat team leader (a sergeant) in the rear. The positioning of the lieutenant in the front of the craft proved disastrous in the initial assault waves, as so many of the young lieutenants were the first men killed when the ramp went down, exposing the craft hold to German machine-gun fire. The green brassard (4) on the rifleman in the center is a chemically impregnated panel that would change color if exposed to chemical weapons. There was considerable concern that the Germans would attempt to repel the landings using gas weapons. So the troops in the assault waves wore battledress impregnated with a special (and uncomfortable) gas-resistant substance and carried a gas mask. Rifles were protected by a plastic wrap (5), though some troops removed this before disembarking. Many of the landing craft were crewed by the Coast Guard, one of whom (6) can be seen to the right. (Howard Gerrard)

with the German beach fortifications. Major Bingham later said that the tanks of the 743rd Tank Battalion had "saved the day. They shot the hell out of the Germans and got the hell shot out of them."

In the 16th RCT sector to the east, Easy Red held out the most promise since there were a few M4A1 tanks from the 741st Tank Battalion providing covering fire, and this area included the only major gap through the obstacles. Company G came in first in the second wave and suffered 30 per cent casualties before reaching the shingle. But in contrast to the first wave, this company was still functional. Company H, 116th RCT landed late a little further west and took heaviest casualties in those boat sections landing nearest the E-1 draw. Three more companies

DOG RED BEACH, 0740HRS (pages 60–61)

The 29th Division's assistant commander, Brigadier General Norman "Dutch" Cota (1), and the 116th Infantry commander, Colonel Canham, landed on Dog White with the second assault wave. They found the troops from the first wave leaderless due to the heavy losses among officers and NCOs. Canham moved westward, prodding his 116th Infantry troops along Dog White to move forward, while Cota headed eastward along Dog White and Dog Red. Cota cajoled the troops, "Don't die on the beaches, die up on the bluff if you have to die. But get off the beaches or you're sure to die!" On meeting Captain John Raaen of the 5th Rangers nearby, he uttered the phrase that would go down in Ranger legend "We're counting on you Rangers to lead the way!" Here Cota is seen talking to some soldiers from the 116th Infantry (2), distinguished by the blue and gray divisional insignia painted on their helmets and worn as a patch on the left shoulder above the rank insignia. To the right are two soldiers from the 5th Rangers (3), evident from the yellow rhomboid painted on the back of their helmets. The 29th Division rifleman in the right of the scene can be seen still wearing the olive green anti-gas brassard (4) and he still carries the chemical protective mask bag (5) on his chest, as does the lieutenant left of Cota. The weapons of many of the GIs had become fouled with sand or seawater during the chaotic landings and the rifleman is attempting to clean his using a toothbrush. On the ground to the right of Cota is a set of bangalore torpedoes (6). These were tubes filled with high explosive that would be joined end to end, and then pushed under wire obstructions. Once in place, they would be detonated to clear a path through the wire. A helmet belonging to a member of one of the Engineer Special Brigades, with its distinctive crescent marking (7), lies on the beach behind Cota. Around 0750hrs, small groups of soldiers from Company C, 1st Battalion, 116th Infantry began moving through a gap in the seawall towards the bluff in an area out of sight of the German machine-gun teams. A private placed a bangalore torpedo under a wire obstruction blocking their path but was killed by sniper fire. A platoon leader, Lieutenant Stanley Schwartz, replaced him and detonated the charge, blowing a wide gap. The first man trying to run through the gap was hit by the sniper and his agonized cries demoralized the troops following. Realizing that the advance was faltering, Cota raced through the gap, shouting back: "C'mon! If an old buzzard like me can do that so can you!" The infantry, with Cota at the lead, waded through tall reeds and marsh grass at the base of the bluffs, finally finding their way to the bluffs. It was the first advance off the beach in the 116th RCT sector. (Howard Gerrard)

from 1/116th Infantry landed between 0740 and 0800, followed by two more from 3/116th Infantry. By 0800hrs there were elements of eight infantry companies on Fox Green beach, mainly concentrated in the area where the gaps in the obstacles had been made between the E-1 and E-3 draws. Several defensive positions were created behind the protection of shingle, and some light machine-guns and 60mm mortars were in action. Company G began another wary advance through the minefields at the base of the bluff and eventually managed to join Spalding's group from Co. E on the crest. Company A tried to follow but suffered heavy losses after wandering into a minefield. These scattered units spent most of the morning advancing slowly southward and dealing with German snipers. Strongpoint WN64 was cleared around 1000hrs although a lone pillbox at the head of the draw remained in German control until the evening.

Further to the east, strongpoint WN60 was captured by Co. L around 0900hrs the first of the defensive positions to fall. The companies from 3/116th RCT began to push further into the F-1 draw towards the village of Cabourg but were halted by the WN63 strongpoint.

The command post for the 16th RCT landed around 0820hrs on Easy Red, along with the much-needed regimental medical section. Colonel George Taylor gathered the battalion and company commanders together and prodded them to get their troops off the beach. "Two kinds of people are staying on the beach, the dead and those who are going to die – now let's get the hell out of here!" Taylor continued down the beach urging the infantrymen forward. At 1100hrs Col. Taylor ordered the decimated 741st Tank Battalion to shift all of its tanks to attack the fortifications in the E-3 Colleville draw. Three M4A1 tanks entered the draw and two were knocked out in duels with the anti-tank guns in the bunkers. Besides the tanks, the engineers' D-7 armored bulldozers were very active in trying to clear beach obstacles to assist the infantry in their attacks.

This photograph was taken after the war looking directly into the D-3 Les Moulins draw. Several of the small structures at the opening of the draw were added after the landings. The numerous bunkers that so effectively resisted the US advance down the access road are difficult to identify due to their small size. (MHI)

From the perspective of General Kraiss, the situation on Omaha Beach was far less worrying than that on neighboring Gold Beach, where British tanks had already comprehensively penetrated the defenses by early morning. Since his division was committed to defending the western side of Gold Beach as well as Omaha Beach, he decided to commit his reserves to stemming the more dangerous British advances. At 0835hrs he asked permission from the 84th Corps HQ to shift all of Kampfgruppe Meyer to the eastern sector against the British, with the exception of the single battalion already promised for the repulse of the American penetrations in front of Colleville. Corps headquarters agreed with this plan. Shortly after these decisions had been made the reports from Omaha Beach began to give cause for concern as US troops continued to penetrate over the bluffs. At 0915hrs GR.916 reported that WN65 to WN68 and WN70 had been captured. From east to west these strongpoints stretched from the west shoulder of the E-1 St Laurent draw across to the west side of the D-3 Les Moulins draw. In fact only WN70 had been abandoned due to the presence of Gen Cota's force. The battalion from Kampfgruppe Meyer due to make the counter-attack towards Colleville had not yet returned from its dawn odyssey to the west.

STALEMATE ON THE BEACH

Although the first penetrations of the German defensive line were well under way by 0900hrs, the Operation Neptune plan was already hours behind schedule. The inability of the Gap Assault Teams to clear and mark sufficient paths through the beach obstructions had caused considerable problems when the tide turned after 0800hrs. There were too few safe approaches to the beach for landing craft and those exits that had been cleared were soon jammed with vehicles that could not move off the beach. At 0830hrs the beachmaster ordered that no landing craft with vehicles should land. Even the troop-laden LCT and LCIs could find no marked lanes to enter, so around mid-morning landings ground to a gradual halt. The senior commanders offshore did not appreciate the status of the forces on the beach due to the loss of so many radios during the landings as well as the generally chaotic situation on the beach. However, the evidence of heavy casualties and

As the assault on Omaha Beach seemed to stall in early morning, Navy destroyers came to the rescue, moving perilously close to shore to provide fire support. This photo, taken from the battleship USS *Texas*, shows one of the destroyers firing at shore targets on D-Day morning. (NARA)

burning equipment, evident even from offshore, allowed little doubt that the landing was in jeopardy.

Realizing that the landing was in peril, around 0800hrs the destroyers began moving dangerously close to shore to provide more fire support to the beleaguered troops. Around 0830hrs USS *McCook* arrived off Vierville and began pounding the D-1 Vierville draw as well as the WN73 strongpoint on Pointe-et-Raz-de-la-Percée that had been inflicting so many casualties on Charlie and Dog Green beaches. After about 15 minutes of fire one of the gun emplacements on the cliff fell into the sea and the other exploded. Around 0950hrs Adm Bryant radioed the destroyers "Get on them men! Get on them! They're raising hell with the men on the beach, and we can't have any more of that! We

The critical link between the army units ashore and the navy destroyers were the Naval Shore Fire Control Parties. One is seen in operation using an SCR-284 with hand-operated generator while the soldier to the right is using an SCR-586 handie-talkie. (NARA)

must stop it!" By 1030hrs the *McCook* took up stations a mere 1,300 yards from shore, in only three fathoms of water, and spent most of the day firing at targets of opportunity. Starting around 0800hrs, USS *Carmick* began a pass offshore from Pointe-et-Raz-de-la-Percée towards Fox Red, eventually approaching within 900yds of shore. With only intermittent contact with shore fire-control parties, the destroyer was close enough that the officers watched where tanks and infantry were firing, and then responded with their own 5in. gunfire. Near the D-3 Les Moulins draw, a tank from the 743rd Tank Battalion began engaging targets on the bluff and then the destroyer eliminated the target with 5in. gunfire. When Bingham's small detachment became trapped in the house at the base of the draw, the *Carmick* began smashing up the WN68 and WN66 strongpoints overlooking the draw. USS *Carmick* was soon joined by USS *Doyle*, which spent much of the day shelling the D-3 Les Moulins draw area. In one of the more famous incidents Adm Bryant ordered the USS *Emmons* to eliminate a German artillery spotter in the steeple of the Colleville church, toppling the belfry with the 13th round. Several other

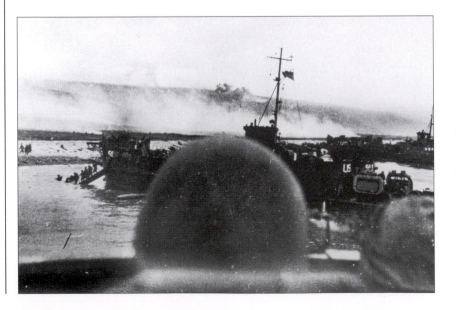

destroyers took part in fire-support missions during the course of the day and they provided what little artillery support was available to the army. One of Gerow's first messages to Bradley after arriving on the beach later in the day was "Thank God for the Navy!"

In spite of the beachmaster's cancellation of any further vehicle landings after 0830hrs, there was a dire need to reinforce the infantry ashore. The next two regiments scheduled to land were the 115th RCT from the 29th Division and the 18th RCT from the 1st Division. These regiments were already onboard the larger LCI(L) "Elsies" and began moving towards the beach around 1000hrs, very behind schedule. The 115th RCT was supposed to land around the D-3 Les Moulins draw, but fire from that area was still so intense the landing site was shifted eastward towards the E-1 St Laurent draw. Not only was this area less subject to German fire but the 115th could follow behind the penetrations already made in this sector. Although there was some sporadic mortar fire during the landings, the regiment suffered relatively light casualties. The WN65 strongpoint on the western side of the draw had been mostly eliminated when G/116th Infantry had advanced over the bluff and tanks and destroyer fire reduced WN64. The 2/115th RCT had to clear a few remaining defenses in WN64, but by 1130hrs the E-1 St Laurent draw had been opened. As a result the 1st and 2nd Battalions, 115th Infantry actually advanced through the draw, while the 3/115th Infantry advanced over the bluff behind the WN64 strongpoint. The Engineer Special Brigade moved into action with bulldozers around 1200 and the E-1 St Laurent draw became the single most important exit route from the beachhead on D-Day.

The situation for the 18th RCT proved somewhat more complicated. Although a gap in the beach obstacles had been made on the eastern side of Easy Red beach, it was poorly marked and by late morning the obstacles were completely submerged. The strongpoints around the E-3 Colleville draw had still not been silenced. For nearly two hours the LCIs carrying the 18th RCT had tried in vain to find clear channels to the

LCI-83 carrying troops of the 20th Engineer Battalion first tried landing at 0830hrs but was unable to do so, transferring some of the troops to shore via LCVPs. Another attempt around 1115hrs, seen here, was more successful but the craft was struck by an artillery round, killing seven and damaging a ramp. Two of the M4A1 tanks of Company A, 741st Tank Battalion can be seen further down the beach. (NARA)

A view from Easy Red beach eastward towards Fox Green and the E-3 Colleville draw shows an LCVP from the *Samuel Chase* in the foreground, and the damaged LCI-553 behind. On the beach are several vehicles including a few tanks from the 741st Tank Battalion. (NARA)

beach. Finally, around 1100hrs the two young skippers on LCT-30 and LCI-554 decided to try to crash through the obstructions and they headed in to Fox Green beach under a hail of gunfire. They began to engage the German gun pits with their own 20mm cannon and .50cal machine-guns and one of the nearby destroyers moved over to provide fire support. Both craft made it to the beach safely and disembarked their troops. LCT-30 was so smashed up by gunfire that it had to be abandoned. LCI-554 managed to pull away from the beach, evacuating a number of wounded at the same time. The example of these two craft convinced other LCI skippers to make an attempt and within moments the shoreline was again swarming with landing craft and the 18th RCT was finally ashore. Casualties were relatively light but a total of 22 LCVPs, two LCIs, and four LCTs were put out of action by beach obstacles while carrying the 18th RCT ashore.

From the German perspective, the defense of Omaha Beach appeared to be holding. Telephone connections to GR.916 were severed at 0855hrs and contact was intermittent through the day. At 1140hrs GR.726 reported that the E-1 St Laurent draw had been breached. However, General Kraiss' attention was focused on neighboring Gold Beach as a result of the rapid advance of British units there. At 1225hrs 84th Corps agreed to transfer the 30th Mobile Brigade to the landing area to be committed opposite Gold Beach. At 1235hrs GR.726 reported that Colleville had fallen into American hands, which was only partly true, and that WN61 on the eastern side of the E-3 Colleville draw was occupied by US troops, which was not true. Through the morning Kraiss had received reports that various strongpoints had fallen to the Americans, to learn moments later that in fact they had not been lost, their communications had simply been cut. He was completely unaware of the penetrations around Vierville by the 116th RCT. By late morning Kraiss concluded that the Allied plan was a two-pronged attack on Bayeux with one arm of the assault emanating out

of the St Laurent/Colleville area and the other out of the British sector. Resources to blunt the attack in the Grandcamps/Omaha Beach sector were limited. He ordered the 14 PzJg 38(t) Ausf. M Marder III tank-destroyers of his anti-tank battalion forward as well as 7/GR.916, which was stationed south of the beach near Trevieres. These forces converged on the area behind the D-3 Les Moulins draw around noon. In the sector south of the St Laurent and Colleville draws he alerted the 5/GR.916 to move forward from its barracks in Surrain and also directed the II/GR.915 from Kampfgruppe Meyer to conduct the counter-attack that had been delayed by the difficulties in moving to the beach. By early afternoon Kraiss believed that the situation on Omaha Beach was under control and at 1335hrs he contacted 84th Corps with the news that the invading forces had been thrown back into the sea except at Colleville, but that his forces were counter-attacking there. This report was forwarded to Army Group B and was one of the few bright spots in view of the dire circumstances on the other Normandy beaches.

Although out of touch with Kraiss and the divisional headquarters, companies of GR.916 were firmly holding defensive positions behind the bluffs, mainly along the road that paralleled the beach. The American infiltrations at this time were not strong enough to overcome these defenses and there were numerous skirmishes through the early afternoon.

The senior US commanders waiting anxiously on ships off the coast were even more confused about the real situation than were the German commanders. Although the situation in the late morning was actually improving on the beach, the news arriving on board the ships reflected the despair of mid-morning. Bradley dispatched an aide by DUKW towards the beach, who sent back alarming reports of the congestion, casualties, and disorder along the beach, concluding at 1130 that "Disaster lies ahead." In fact, by late morning the situation on Omaha Beach was rapidly improving. The reinforcements from the 115th and 18th RCTs, although slow in moving off the beach, solidified

the four penetrations over the dunes. The naval gunfire from the destroyers was wreaking havoc with the German strongpoints and, furthermore, the German gunners were running out of ammunition after the intense firing of earlier in the morning. While the situation was far from secure, the momentum was shifting in favor of the American assault.

THE RANGERS AT POINTE-DU-HOC

The most isolated skirmish of the morning was fought by the three companies of the 2nd Rangers under LtCol James Rudder that had been sent to silence the guns on Pointe-du-Hoc. The rocky promontory had been thoroughly pulverized by naval gunfire and bombers prior to the mission, including 698 tons of bombs in the early morning hours. The assault force of about 200 Rangers were loaded into ten British LCAs escorted by several other craft. The mission began badly when the waterlogged LCA carrying the Co. D commander sank in the assembly area along with a supply craft. The remainder of the flotilla, led by a Royal Navy Fairmile motor-launch and escorted by a pair of British LCS fire-support craft, set off for the objective. The guide boat became disoriented and led the flotilla towards Pointe-et-Raz-de-la-Percée to the east of Pointe-du-Hoc before Rudder realized the mistake and ordered the flotilla westward. The navigation error cost the Rangers about 40 minutes and they had to run a gauntlet of fire from the cliffs. A DUKW and an LCS were sunk by 20mm cannon fire. During the lull between the naval bombardment and the arrival of the landing craft, the German garrison on top of Pointe-du-Hoc exited their concrete bunkers and made their way to the edge of the cliffs.

The nine LCAs landed along the eastern side of Pointe-du-Hoc, with the crews setting off the grappling rockets on touchdown. The early-

A section from the 2nd Rangers is seen loaded in the hold of their LCA in Weymouth, England, before setting out across the Channel for Pointe-du-Hoc. The diamond-shaped Ranger insignia can be seen on the back of several helmets. There is a BAR gunner to the left and a bazooka gunner to the far right. (NARA)

The preliminary naval bombardment of Pointe-du-Hoc collapsed a large section of the eastern cliff onto the beach. This reduced the height that the Rangers had to climb to reach the top of the promontory in this area. (NARA)

morning naval bombardment by the battleship USS *Texas* had caused a large slab of cliff to fall off, creating a 40ft mound of spoil. This was both a blessing and a curse. It prevented the DUKWs from deploying their scaling ladders, but nearly half the height of the cliff could be climbed without ropes or ladders. German troops began appearing along the edge of the cliffs as the Rangers landed, firing small arms, and causing about 15 casualties. The destroyer *Satterlee* came in close to shore and swept the cliff top with fire, forcing the German garrison back into the shell craters and bunkers. Within five minutes of landing, the first

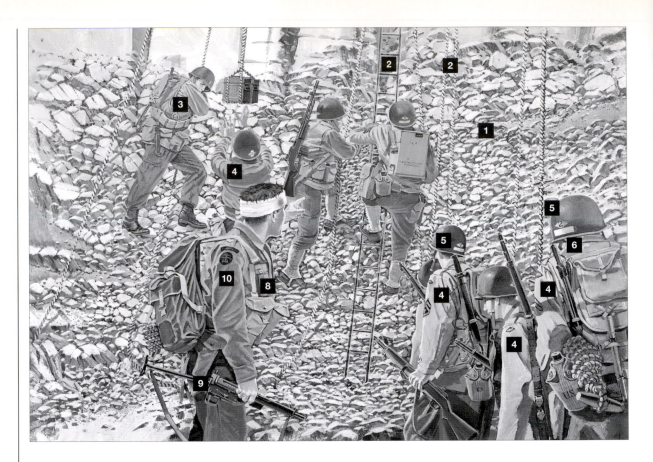

THE 2ND RANGERS AT POINTE-DU-HOC (pages 72–73)

The original plan for the Ranger landing at Pointe-du-Hoc was to land two companies on the east side of the cliffs, and one on the west side. Due to the delays caused by a navigational error all three companies landed on the east side. LCA-888 carrying a section from Company D landed along the cliffs where the preparatory naval bombardment had collapsed a large slab of the rock-face, creating a heap of spoil (1) about 40ft high. This spoil and the shell craters along the beach prevented the DUKW amphibious trucks from placing their ladders up against the cliff. But the spoil allowed the Rangers from Company D to climb almost half way up the cliff without the need for ropes or assault ladders (2). The first ropes were launched over the edge of the cliff using rocket-propelled grappling hooks. Once the first fire teams had reached the top, they dropped additional ropes down the cliff to the troops below. In this scene, the Rangers are continuing to climb the cliffs after the first teams have established a toehold above. Many of the Rangers, like the first wave of assault troops, wore the distinctive assault jacket (3), best seen on the lieutenant at the left. The Rangers at the right are wearing the distinctive insignia of the Rangers including the blue and yellow Ranger rhomboid patch (4) on their left shoulder and yellow/orange rhomboid with the battalion number superimposed in black (5) painted on the rear of the M1 steel helmet. The horizontal white stripe on the back of the helmet (6) is a standard US Army marking, indicating an NCO. Officers' helmets were painted with a vertical white stripe (7). The British Commando (8) with the bandaged head is serving as a liaison with the Rangers for the mission. He is armed with a Sten gun (9) and wears British battledress with the distinctive Commando insignia (10) on his shoulder. (Howard Gerrard)

A view up the cliff showing where many of the Rangers climbed on D-Day. This photograph was taken by a navy photographer a few days after the landings. (NARA)

Rangers were on top of the cliffs. The promontory was a lunar landscape of deep bomb and shell craters that provided the Rangers with ample cover. But the terrain was so pockmarked that the Rangers had a difficult time assembling or communicating. By the time the main body of Rangers ascended the cliff, the survivors of the German garrison had withdrawn into the surviving bunkers. Prior to the bombardment the German garrison on Pointe-du-Hoc consisted of about 125 troops of the 716th Division manning the defensive positions, as the 85 artillerymen had withdrawn off the point three days before.

There had been some hints the night before the landing that Allied intelligence had learned that the guns had been withdrawn. When the Rangers reached the casemates they found that this was indeed the case. The only "guns" on Pointe-du-Hoc were a number of dummies made from timber. At least two significant concentrations of German troops remained on the point for much of the morning, the most dangerous being an anti-aircraft position at the southwest corner of the artillery position that resisted repeated Ranger attacks. The observation bunker at the tip of the point was defended by a handful of German troops and there were several small groups of German soldiers in the ruins of the ammunition and troop bunkers. A German strongpoint on a cliff to the east continued to rake the point with harassing fire for much of the morning until a British destroyer spotted it and blasted it into the sea.

Small groups of Rangers gradually set out southward to secure the point and about 50 men reached the highway by 0800hrs after a firefight near two German defensive positions on the southern edge of the base. Small patrols infiltrated south through the farm fields looking for the missing guns. A two-man patrol finally found them, completely unguarded but ready to fire, in an apple orchard in Criqueville-en-Bessin about 600yds south of the battery positions. They were pointed towards Utah beach, with ammunition at the ready. The first patrol placed thermite grenades in two guns and smashed the sights, and further damage was done when a second patrol arrived with more grenades. The Rangers had accomplished their mission.

The other elements of the Provisional Ranger Group still at sea remained unaware of Rudder's success. Although a message at 0725hrs that the Rangers were up the cliffs was acknowledged, a second message at 0745 that the point had been taken was not acknowledged. As a result of Rudder's force landing 40 minutes late, the remainder of the Provisional Ranger Force assumed that the mission had failed and went ashore with the 116th RCT at 0730hrs. This would pose a major problem to Rudder's force as by 0830 it was barely at company strength and attracting an increasing amount of German attention. About 60 Rangers remained in and around the point, establishing a lightly defended skirmish line near the southern edge of the battery positions. At the same time Rudder sent out a number of small patrols, about a half-dozen men each, to scout and clear out isolated pockets of German troops who had withdrawn from the battery positions due to the bombardment.

The headquarters of the German 352nd Infantry Division knew about the attack almost from the outset, but the news was not particularly alarming in view of the disturbing events elsewhere. At 0805hrs GR.916 reported to divisional headquarters that a "weak force" had penetrated into Pointe-du-Hoc and that a platoon from 9/GR.726 was being sent to

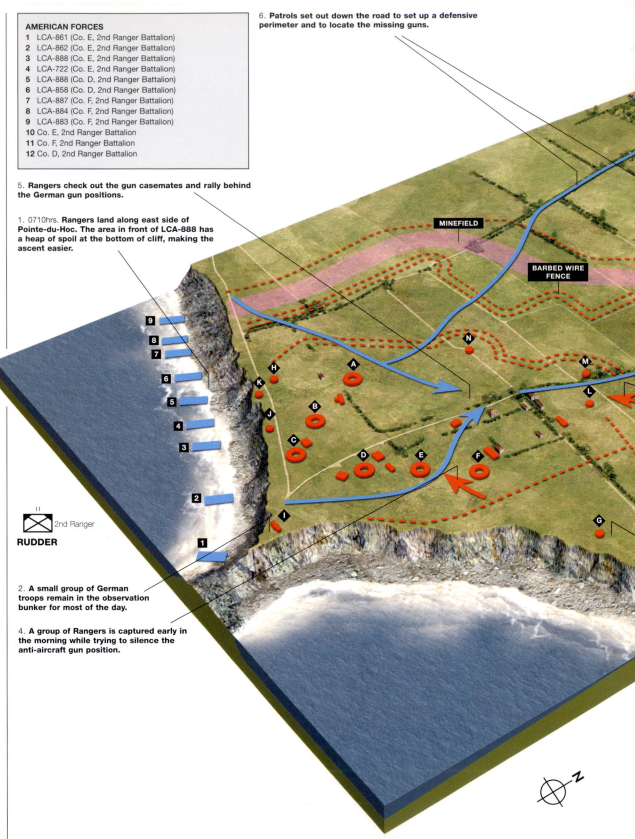

6. **Patrols set out down the road to set up a defensive perimeter and to locate the missing guns.**

AMERICAN FORCES
1. LCA-861 (Co. E, 2nd Ranger Battalion)
2. LCA-862 (Co. E, 2nd Ranger Battalion)
3. LCA-888 (Co. E, 2nd Ranger Battalion)
4. LCA-722 (Co. E, 2nd Ranger Battalion)
5. LCA-888 (Co. D, 2nd Ranger Battalion)
6. LCA-858 (Co. D, 2nd Ranger Battalion)
7. LCA-887 (Co. F, 2nd Ranger Battalion)
8. LCA-884 (Co. F, 2nd Ranger Battalion)
9. LCA-883 (Co. F, 2nd Ranger Battalion)
10. Co. E, 2nd Ranger Battalion
11. Co. F, 2nd Ranger Battalion
12. Co. D, 2nd Ranger Battalion

5. **Rangers check out the gun casemates and rally behind the German gun positions.**

1. 0710hrs. **Rangers land along east side of Pointe-du-Hoc. The area in front of LCA-888 has a heap of spoil at the bottom of cliff, making the ascent easier.**

MINEFIELD

BARBED WIRE FENCE

2nd Ranger

RUDDER

2. **A small group of German troops remain in the observation bunker for most of the day.**

4. **A group of Rangers is captured early in the morning while trying to silence the anti-aircraft gun position.**

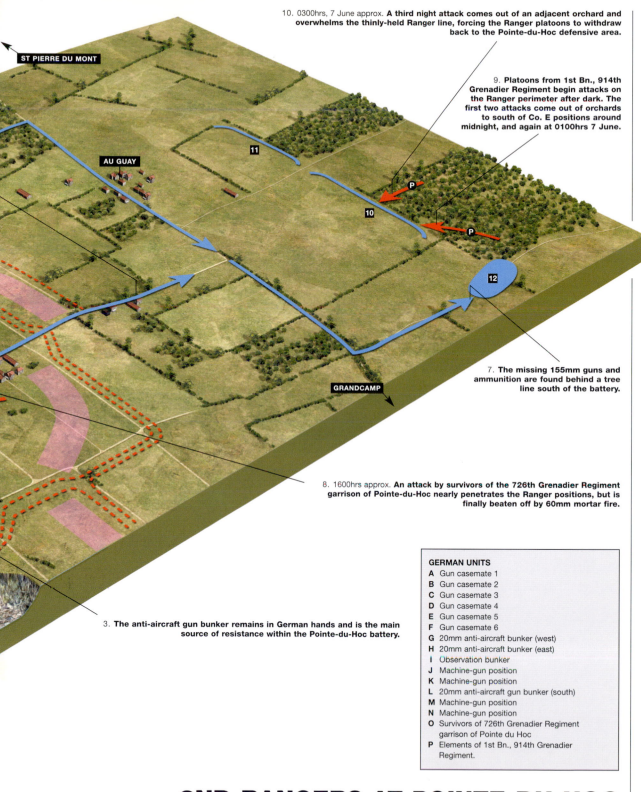

10. 0300hrs, 7 June approx. **A third night attack comes out of an adjacent orchard and overwhelms the thinly-held Ranger line, forcing the Ranger platoons to withdraw back to the Pointe-du-Hoc defensive area.**

9. **Platoons from 1st Bn., 914th Grenadier Regiment begin attacks on the Ranger perimeter after dark. The first two attacks come out of orchards to south of Co. E positions around midnight, and again at 0100hrs 7 June.**

ST PIERRE DU MONT

AU GUAY

11

10

P

P

12

GRANDCAMP

7. The missing 155mm guns and ammunition are found behind a tree line south of the battery.

8. 1600hrs approx. **An attack by survivors of the 726th Grenadier Regiment garrison of Pointe-du-Hoc nearly penetrates the Ranger positions, but is finally beaten off by 60mm mortar fire.**

3. The anti-aircraft gun bunker remains in German hands and is the main source of resistance within the Pointe-du-Hoc battery.

GERMAN UNITS	
A	Gun casemate 1
B	Gun casemate 2
C	Gun casemate 3
D	Gun casemate 4
E	Gun casemate 5
F	Gun casemate 6
G	20mm anti-aircraft bunker (west)
H	20mm anti-aircraft bunker (east)
I	Observation bunker
J	Machine-gun position
K	Machine-gun position
L	20mm anti-aircraft gun bunker (south)
M	Machine-gun position
N	Machine-gun position
O	Survivors of 726th Grenadier Regiment garrison of Pointe du Hoc
P	Elements of 1st Bn., 914th Grenadier Regiment.

2ND RANGERS AT POINTE-DU-HOC

0710hrs 6 June–0300hrs 7 June 1944, viewed from the northwest showing the successful assault on the Pointe du Hoc battery by Lieutenant Colonel James E. Rudder's 2nd Ranger Battalion.

counter-attack. The German resistance forced the Rangers to set up a defensive line south and east of the Pointe-du-Hoc fortifications. The first significant counter-attack by 9/GR.726 came out of St Pierre-du-Mont to the eastern side of the Ranger defensive line in the early afternoon. It was repulsed by rifle fire. A more dangerous attack began around 1600hrs on the western edge of the defenses near the anti-aircraft pit. This attack was finally broken up by the Ranger's sole surviving 60mm mortar. The V Corps headquarters knew nothing of the fate of the Rangers until the afternoon when a message was passed via the *Satterlee*, which remained off the point for most of the day providing fire support. The message was simple and to the point: "Located Pointe du Hoe – mission accomplished – need ammunition and reinforcements – many casualties."

The 2nd Rangers landing at Pointe-du-Hoc were led by Lieutenant Colonel James Rudder. He is seen here at his command post at the edge of the cliff a few days after the landing with an EE-84 signal lamp behind him, which was used to communicate with ships at sea due to the loss of most of the unit's radios. (MHI)

The Rangers on Pointe-du-Hoc remained isolated for most of the day, expecting the planned relief force from the 116th RCT and 5th Rangers to arrive at any time. At dusk around 2100hrs, a patrol of 23 soldiers from Co. A, 5th Rangers led by Lieutenant Charles Parker made their way into the defensive line. Parker's group had been with the force that had made the penetration into Vierville earlier in the day and, facing modest resistance, they gradually infiltrated through German defenses to Pointe-du-Hoc.

In view of the lack of success of GR.726 in overcoming the Rangers, at 1825hrs Gen. Kraiss ordered 1/GR.914 to regain control of Pointe-du-Hoc. Nightfall came late, around 2300hrs, and the Ranger defensive line of about 85 soldiers stretched along a series of hedgerows south of

The 2nd Rangers take a break near the unit headquarters on Pointe-du-Hoc after a relief column from the 116th RCT had reached them on D-Day+2. Note the British Commando in the lower right of the photo. (MHI)

the battery complex and the hamlet of Au Guay. German infantry began probing the defenses shortly after dark and skirmishing began in earnest around 0100hrs. A concerted German attack around 0300hrs overwhelmed a portion of the defensive line, capturing 20 Rangers. This forced the Rangers in the outlying positions to withdraw back from the orchards and into the battery positions behind the road. By dawn on D+1 Rudder's force had been reduced to 90 Rangers capable of bearing arms and several dozen wounded. Naval gunfire kept the 1/GR.914 at bay and in the afternoon a landing craft finally arrived with provisions, ammunition and a relief platoon. But throughout D+1 the Rangers on Pointe-du-Hoc could do little more than hold on for the relief force to arrive. During the night of D+1 a patrol from the relief force arrived, by which time the 116th RCT had reached St Pierre-du-Mont only 1,000yds away. The relief of the Rangers at Pointe-du-Hoc finally came on the morning of D+2, spearheaded by tanks of the 743rd Tank Battalion.

CONSOLIDATING THE BEACHHEAD

The senior US commanders did not have an accurate appreciation of the situation on the beach until well into the afternoon of D-Day. The first favorable reports by Col Talley of the Forward Information Detachment did not arrive at Gerow's V Corps HQ on the USS *Ancon* until 1225hrs and spoke vaguely of "men advancing up slopes" and "men believed to be ours on skyline." At 1309hrs Talley sent the first optimistic report back to the ships: "Troops formerly pinned down on beaches Easy Red, Easy Green, Fox Red advancing up heights behind beaches."

As the second group of regiments landed in late morning, the situation along the beach was shifting from total chaos to mere disorder. By noon the Engineer Special Brigades had enough troops ashore to begin the complicated task of preparing the beachhead for subsequent waves of troops and equipment. Some significant portions of the beach, especially in the Easy Red sector, were relatively free of small arms fire although still subject to occasional mortar and artillery fire. The beaches were littered with the dead and wounded, smashed and burning equipment and a significant traffic jam of troops and vehicles unable to move off the beach. None of the draws had been cleared sufficiently to permit traffic off the beach and the troops moving inland were all walking over the bluffs.

One of the engineers' first tasks was to finish removing the beach obstructions. High tide was around 1100hrs and then the sea began to recede, making it easier to tackle the obstacle problem. The areas along the bluffs were still heavily mined and these minefields had to be cleared to permit troops to safely pass southward. The worst beaches of the morning had been Charlie and Dog Green to the west. Like the infantry landing there, the engineers had taken heavy casualties. By late morning C/121st Engineers had landed along with bulldozers and explosives. Between 1200 and 1300hrs navy shore fire-control parties directed four salvoes from the battleship USS *Texas* against surviving bunkers in the D-1 Vierville draw. Stunned by the barrage, about 30 surviving German soldiers exited the bunkers and surrendered. A few moments later Gen. Cota walked down the draw from the other side to try to get more troops moving to Vierville. At 1400, as he watched, the engineers breached the

The first exit to be opened was the E-1 St Laurent draw, locally known as the Ruquet valley. This was the site of the first penetration of the bluffs in the 16th RCT sector by Lieutenant Spalding's group towards the right side of this photo. Here we see a column of German prisoners of war evacuating their wounded to landing craft on the shore for transit back to camps in the UK. The area under the blimp was the site of the WN65 strongpoint. (NARA)

anti-tank wall there with a half-ton of explosives. The road to Vierville was finally open around 1800hrs although still subject to artillery fire. The D-3 Les Moulins draw remained the most stubborn of the defenses and no progress was made until late evening when it was declared open at 2000hrs. The E-1 St Laurent draw had been one of the first German strongpoints overcome in the morning, but progress was slow in clearing the many minefields, filling in anti-tank ditches, clearing barbed wire obstructions and removing accumulated debris. Under continual sniper fire, bulldozers plowed a new road up the bluff west of the draw by 1300hrs. The availability of a road off the beach led the beachmaster to open Easy Red and Easy Green to vehicles again, the first DUKWs arriving around 1400hrs.

The E-3 Colleville draw was strongly defended and the last pillbox was not silenced by tank fire until 1630hrs. The draw remained dangerous through most of the evening as it was registered for artillery fire, with salvoes arriving every 15–20 minutes. Engineer work to clear the

Beached landing craft and debris clog the shores of Fox Green beach at the end of D-Day while medical teams set about the task of recovering the dead and the wounded. (NARA)

obstructions at the front of the draw began around 2000hrs when artillery fire slackened. Tanks began moving through the draw around 0100hrs on D+1, but wheeled vehicles did not use the exit until dawn. By the evening of D-Day the engineers had fully cleared 13 of the 16 gaps that planners had expected to be open after the first wave landed. About 35 per cent of the beach obstacles had been cleared as well.

Efforts to land artillery on the beach for fire support proved frustrating. The field artillery battalions attached to the infantry regiments had their 105mm howitzers on DUKWs. But these amphibious trucks were heavily loaded and in rough seas they began to ship water. All but one of the DUKWs of the 111th Field Artillery Battalion (116th RCT) sank. The 7th Field Artillery Battalion (16th RCT) lost six on the way in and the remaining six were unable to land in mid-morning due to the beach

Engineers from 5th Engineers Special Brigade come ashore from LCT-538 on Easy Red around 1130hrs. The engineers had the distinctive crescent marking on their helmets as seen here. The photographer who took this photo, Captain Herman Wall of the 165th Photographic Company, was wounded shortly after this picture was taken. (NARA)

Anti-tank ditches at the base of the bluffs were also turned into aid stations on the afternoon and evening of D-Day. Once stabilized, the wounded were sent back to ships for further medical treatment or evacuation to Britain. (NARA)

congestion. The two armored field artillery battalions with M7 105mm self-propelled howitzers participated in the early bombardment from offshore and had no more luck landing. Five of the LCTs of the 58th Armored Field Artillery Battalion struck mines or were sunk and the 62nd Armored Field Artillery Battalion was unable to land. The 7th Field Artillery Battalion plus a single 105mm howitzer from the 111th Field Artillery Battalion fired their first mission from the beach at 1615hrs against German machine-gun nests near Colleville. Six M7 105mm self-propelled howitzers from the 62nd Armored Field Artillery Battalion finally made it ashore by 1830, but were not ready for action on D-Day. Seven M7 105mm self-propelled howitzers of the 58th Armored Field Artillery Battalion arrived in the afternoon and were sent to support the fighting near St Laurent. In total, five artillery battalions were eventually landed on D-Day, but lost 26 of their 60 howitzers and saw very little use.

One of the most valuable types of vehicle on the beach in the first few hours of D-Day was the D-7 armored bulldozer. These were used by the engineers to clear beach obstructions, fill in anti-tank ditches and perform a multitude of other tasks, whilst constantly under fire. This one is seen in a Norman town a few days after D-Day. (NARA)

THE BATTLES FOR THE VILLAGES

Throughout the afternoon a series of skirmishes raged all along the coastal road, centered on the small villages located behind the bluffs. The first of these to be taken was Vierville on the western side of Omaha Beach. The American control of the Vierville sector remained precarious throughout D-Day due to the extremely heavy losses suffered by the units landing on Charlie and Dog Green beaches and the diversion of the reinforcing wave of the 115th RCT to beaches further east. In addition, the German 352nd Infantry Division had an unbloodied regiment west of Pointe-et-Raz-de-la-Percée. A company from the 5th Rangers and 116th Infantry headed west out of Vierville around noon but were stopped by German defensive positions. The remainder of the Ranger force arrived by late afternoon but the 116th RCT commander, Col Canham, decided against pushing on to Pointe-du-Hoc that day due to the weakness of his force. This was a realistic assessment as the German forces opposite Vierville were the strongest in any sector. To the immediate south of Vierville was the III/GR.726, which was reinforced by elements of the 352nd Infantry Division's engineer battalion and the 7/GR.916 later in the day. To the west were two companies of GR.726 and a battalion of GR.914, reinforced late in the day by a battalion from the 30th Mobile Brigade.

With the D-1 Vierville draw finally cleared by late afternoon, the surviving 17 tanks of the 743rd Tank Battalion moved into Vierville for the night. US tank losses on D-Day were 79 and if it had not been for the four reserve tanks landed later in the day, the 741st Tank Battalion would have been without tanks. Several of the disabled tanks were put back into service over the next few days.

The advance towards St Laurent in the center had progressed more slowly even though there were about five battalions of US infantry in the immediate area. The hedgerows and orchards made the area well suited for defense and the US units were scattered and uncoordinated. To deal with the US attack, Kraiss ordered his dozen 75mm PzJg 38(t) Ausf. M Marder III tank-destroyers forward to support local counter-attacks by the 7/GR.916. The tank-destroyers were spotted by naval observation aircraft and pummeled by naval gunfire well south of the beach. Their attack came to an end before reaching US lines. The two companies of 3/116th Infantry fought a number of skirmishes with the newly arrived 7/GR.916 and their advance slowed as a result. In addition, strongpoint WN67 covered the crossroads where the road from the beach intersected the coastal road. Unknown to the 3/116th Infantry, the 2/115th Infantry was advancing southward along the eastern side of St Laurent and spent most of the afternoon skirmishing with German troops inside the village. The area was hit by a naval barrage around dusk, which halted the US attack. Around 1700hrs four M4A1 tanks from the 741st Tank Battalion were ordered through the E-1 St Laurent draw to reinforce the attack on the village but, not finding the infantry, they formed a defensive line on the eastern side of the village. By this time 1/115th Infantry had bypassed St Laurent and bedded down in the fields south of the village. The 2/115th Infantry joined them there by nightfall. The tanks finally linked up with some scattered infantry units, and conducted a few missions with the infantry to clear out snipers and machine-gun nests shortly before nightfall.

Although few field artillery batteries were able to take part in the fighting on D-Day, the 81st Chemical Weapons Battalion landed on D-Day morning, armed with 4.2in. mortars. It was split between the 16th and 116th RCTs and provided the only shore-based artillery support in the morning and early afternoon. (NARA)

Scattered platoons from the 16th Infantry began the fighting for Colleville in mid-morning. Around noon the US forces had coalesced into a force of about 150 men and began moving into the western side of the village. While this was taking place, elements of the II/GR.915 from Kampfgruppe Meyer appeared on the scene and began to reinforce the German positions around Colleville. Company G, 16th Infantry was forced onto the defensive until the arrival of 2/18th Infantry around 1500hrs. This was the counter-attack ordered by Kraiss earlier in the morning but it was not well organized and failed to push back the US penetration as planned. Further American penetration into the village was halted when naval gunfire hit the village in the late afternoon. The 2/18th Infantry made its way south of Colleville, while the three under-strength battalions of the 16th Infantry were deployed in a band along the coastal highway southwest of Colleville. The situation in this area was extremely confused, as not only were the US units facing local attacks by II/GR.915, but numerous small groups of German troops were retreating from the defensive works near the beach and bumping into US patrols.

On the eastern side of the beach, the small village of Le Garde Hameau was taken early in the day and occupied by 3/16th Infantry. When the third regiment of the 1st Infantry Division began arriving later in the day one of its battalions, 1/26th Infantry, was sent through

Company A, 741st Tank Battalion provided the 16th RCT with critical fire support against German strongpoints during the morning of D-Day. This tank, A-13 "Adeline II", was hit on the rear bogie by a 50mm anti-tank gun during fighting against the bunkers in the E-1 St Laurent draw. The tank could still move in spite of the damage, but it could not surmount the seawall to exit the beach. It was later recovered by the battalion's T2 tank recovery vehicle and is seen being towed through Colleville after D-Day for repair. (NARA)

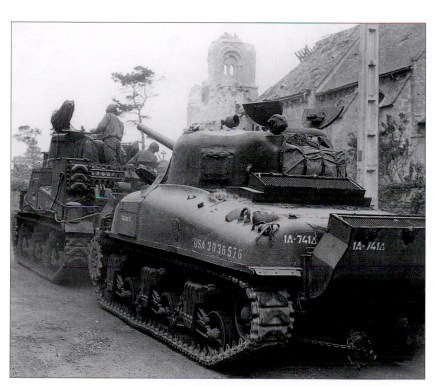

the F-1 draw and bivouacked north of Cabourg, while the other two battalions went over the bluff west of the E-3 Colleville draw to secure the area between the 1st and 29th Divisions between St Laurent and Colleville.

ABOVE **US troops spent the next few days after D-Day clearing up isolated pockets of German troops and snipers in the countryside around the beach. This soldier's choice of a surrender flag was maybe not the best, but seems to have worked! (NARA)**

ABOVE, LEFT **Reinforcements continued to arrive through D-Day and this platoon is seen moving through a mine-cleared lane west of the E-1 St Laurent draw. The engineers marked lanes with white tape as seen here. (NARA)**

OMAHA BEACH IN RETROSPECT

ABOVE **Following the landings, engineers were kept very busy clearing the beaches and the immediate coastal areas of the thousands of mines that the Germans had laid. This engineer is using the standard SCR-625 mine-detector near the beach on 13 June 1944. The painted insignia on his helmet identifies him as belonging to one of the Engineer Special Brigades.**

RIGHT **Dog White beach is littered with shattered vehicles and craft at low tide on the evening of 6 June 1944. The M4 tank, C-13 "Ceaseless" is from Co. C, 743rd Tank Battalion and was disabled on the beach after losing a track. General Cota led the breakthrough in the 116th RCT sector across the bluffs in this area earlier in the morning. (NARA)**

By the end of D-Day, the US Army had a firm toehold on Omaha Beach, clinging to a ragged line about a mile inland from the beach. This fell far short of the plan but was, in view of the serious underestimation of German strength, a significant accomplishment. A total of about 34,200 troops landed at Omaha Beach on D-Day. In spite of the large numbers of troops landed much of this force was still congregated on or near the beach at the end of the day. The assault forces south of the beach were too scattered, disconnected and weak to make a push forward until the next day. The senior US commanders had not expected the landings at Omaha Beach to be difficult. The decisive action would come when the Germans launched a violent counter-attack within a day or two of the landings. In the event, the landings proved to be more costly than expected, but the German counter-attack never materialized.

Precise US casualties for D-Day will never be accurately determined. The V Corps history places the total at 1,190 for the 1st Infantry Division, 743 for the 29th Division and 441 for V Corps troops for a total of 2,374. Of these, 694 were killed, 331 missing and 1,349 wounded. No breakdown is available by rank, but from written reports the casualties amongst the combat leaders – the young majors, captains, lieutenants, and sergeants – had been disproportionately high. The 1st Division later reduced their casualty figures as the missing were gradually located and a total of about 2,000 army casualties is the generally accepted figure for Omaha Beach on D-Day. This exceeded the casualties of all the other beaches combined. There has been a tendency to exaggerate these losses in recent years,

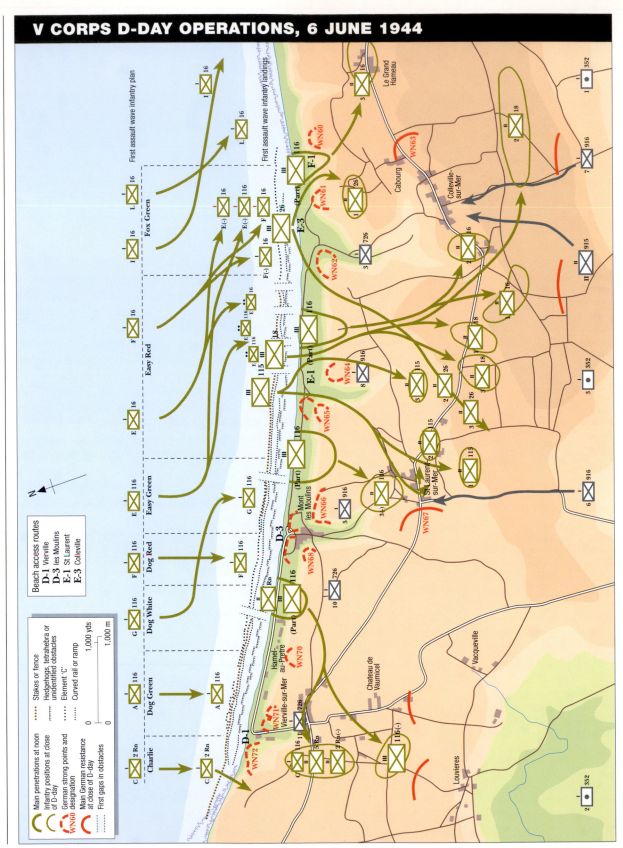

Beach access routes
D-1 Vierville
D-3 les Moulins
E-1 St Laurent
E-3 Colleville

Main penetrations at noon

Infantry positions at close of D-day

German strong points and designation

Main German resistance at close of D-day

First gaps in obstacles

Stakes or fence

Hedgehogs, tetrahedra or unidentified obstacles

Element 'C'

Curved rail or ramp

0   1,000 yds
0   1,000 m

First assault wave infantry plan

First assault wave infantry landings

To stiffen the Normandy defenses, Rommel had pressed obsolete WWI field guns into service including German 77mm guns re-bored to 75mm and Czech Skoda 76.2mm guns. Old or not, these weapons were very effective against exposed infantry on the beaches below. This particular one has taken a direct hit, probably from a tank gun, on the right side of its splinter shield, which has also blown off one of the wheels. (NARA)

especially in view of the difficulty of the assignment. As dreadful as they were it should be remembered that the US Army suffered an average of 1,200 casualties a day during the fighting in Normandy in July 1944. What marked out Omaha Beach from later Normandy fighting was the high level of losses among the first assault waves in such a short period of time. Yet the bloodletting should not obscure the fact that Hitler's vaunted Atlantic Wall had withstood the Allied onslaught for less than a day. The sacrifice at Omaha was the foundation for the forthcoming liberation of France.

The reasons for the high casualties are not difficult to identify. Omaha Beach was much more heavily defended than any other beach and its high bluffs posed a much more substantial defensive obstacle than the relatively flat beaches elsewhere. A classified wartime British study noted that the three beaches in the British/Canadian sector were defended by an average of nine anti-tank guns per beach compared to 30 anti-tank and field guns at Omaha, four mortars per beach compared to six at Omaha and 21 machine-guns compared to 85 at Omaha. In addition Omaha was subjected to fire from two artillery battalions, compared to a battalion or less at most of the other beaches. Finally, the preparatory bombardment of Omaha Beach was shorter than those at the neighboring British/Canadian beaches, in some cases by as much as an hour, as the Omaha landing took place earlier due to tidal variations.

Although the initial bomber attack on Omaha Beach had been a failure, the activity of the Allied air forces over Normandy on D-Day had been extremely effective. The most important consequence of Allied air superiority over the beach was that it gave free rein to Allied bombers and fighter-bombers to isolate German reserves from the beachhead. Movement by any type of motorized transport became difficult or impossible. The US Eighth Air Force conducted 1,729 heavy bomber missions on D-Day and IX Bomber Command added a further 823 medium bomber attacks for a combined total of 5,037 tons of bombs delivered. The Eighth Air Force conducted 1,880 fighter sorties on D-Day and the Ninth Air Force a further 2,065 fighter-bomber missions.

The performance of the US Navy at Omaha Beach had been exemplary. The US Navy, Coast Guard and Royal Navy crews of the landing craft had contended with fearsome difficulties through the day and had landed the force in the face of intense fire. When the landings appeared to falter, the young destroyer skippers skillfully maneuvered in shallow water to bring their vital firepower to bear on the German fortifications. These actions helped turn the tide of the D-Day fighting and Omaha Beach was a combined arms battle in the fullest sense of the term.

The German perspective at the end of D-Day was far more pessimistic than in the afternoon when it appeared that the invasion had been thwarted on Omaha. General Kraiss retained little hope of stemming the Allied forces unless substantial reinforcements arrived. Casualties on D-Day had not been particularly high compared with US losses; about 1,000 men. But his artillery was out of ammunition, his units were thinly spread and no units remained in reserve. He was primarily concerned

The headquarters of the German 352nd Infantry Division got the first clear glimpse of the enormity of the Allied landings in the late morning of D+1 when Colonel Fritz Ziegelmann reached a strongpoint still in German hands on the Pointe-et-Raz-de-la-Percée promontory on the western side of the beach. The scene he saw was something like this, although this view is from the eastern side of the beach. (NARA)

about the breakthrough by British armor in the neighboring Gold Beach sector next to Omaha. The counter-attack by Kampfgruppe Meyer near Bazenville during the afternoon and evening of D-Day had been decisively smashed by the British. Oberstleutnant Meyer had been killed and his three battalions reduced to less than 100 effectives. This consumed the 84th Corps reserve except for the 30th Mobile Brigade, which was being fed in piecemeal to cover gaps in the line. Kraiss did not have a firm idea of the status of Omaha Beach since communication had been lost with most of the forward strongpoints, and his forces along the coastal highway received contradictory stories from the stragglers retreating back from the beachhead strongpoints. Nevertheless, his defensive line opposite Omaha Beach appeared to be holding, which was far better than could be said for the situation on either side of Omaha Beach. The following day, he sent his operations officer to the surviving WN76 strongpoint on Pointe-et-Raz-de-la-Percée. The trip took five hours instead the usual 30 minutes due to Allied aircraft. Oberstleutnant Fritz Ziegelmann later wrote: "The view from WN76 will remain in my memory forever. The sea was like a picture from the Kiel review of the German fleet. Ships of all sorts nestled close together on the beach, and echeloned at sea in depth. And the entire concentration remained there intact without any real interference from the German side! I clearly understood the mood of the German soldier who was pleading for the Luftwaffe. That the German soldiers fought here hard and stubbornly is, and remains, a wonder."

The Luftwaffe, battered by months of Allied air action, played practically no role in the fighting. The commander of Luftflotte 3, Generalfeldmarschall Hugo Sperrle, did not authorize the "Impending Danger West" signal until mid-morning on 6 June 1944, even though his reconnaissance aircraft had spotted the Allied fleets before dawn. As a result, the many fighter units that had been moved inland to avoid Allied fighter sweeps did not return to the forward fields near the Channel until the evening of D-Day. The only Luftwaffe aircraft over the beaches on D-Day were a pair of Fw-190 from I/Jagdgeschwader 26 led by the squadron commander, Oberstlt Josef "Pips" Priller, which took off from Lille around 0800hrs and made a fast pass over the Normandy beaches before landing, out of fuel, at Creil. The units near the coast were able to launch only about 100 daylight sorties on D-Day of which 70 had been by fighters. The Luftwaffe fighters claimed 24 Allied aircraft, but lost 16 fighters in the process. One attempted raid on the beaches by a dozen Ju-88 bombers led to the entire force being shot down. The Luftwaffe attempted to redeem itself with a concerted night attack by the bombers and torpedo-bombers of Fliegerkorps IX, but few of the 175 sorties managed to reach the Allied fleets due to Allied night-fighters and anti-aircraft fire. The Kriegsmarine had even less effect on the landings and its warships and coastal artillery played no role whatsoever at Omaha Beach.

The reaction by higher German commands on D-Day was tentative and indecisive. There was the belief through most of the day that the Normandy landings were a diversion, and not the main invasion. Hitler was reluctant to commit the Panzer reserves and insisted that the landings be crushed with local resources. This indecision would linger through much of June. Rommel began moving the Panzer divisions under his control against the Allied beaches, but none of this force was directed against Omaha Beach. Nor did the Panzers have a decisive impact once deployed over the next few days. Not only was it difficult to move the Panzer divisions forward due to air attack but the area of coastal farmland behind the beaches, known as the *bocage*, was broken up by thick hedges and constricted by a poor road network that made maneuver impossible. The battles in Normandy, especially in the American sectors, would be an infantry battle.

The US V Corps gradually expanded the Omaha beachhead, finally reaching the Aure River and the D-Day objectives two days late. The 352nd Infantry Division continued to offer stiff resistance but the advantage was clearly shifting to the growing American forces. On 9 June V Corps launched its first offensive out of the beachhead, a three-division attack that pushed 12 miles inland and seized the dominating terrain at the Cerisy forest. On 12 June the attack was resumed and the Utah and Omaha beachheads joined by seizing Carentan. By 13 June V Corps had pushed 20 miles beyond the beachhead, linking with both Utah and Gold beaches on either flank. In the neighboring Utah Beach sector Collins' VII Corps faced far less formidable defenses and reached the seaport of Cherbourg on 20 June. But the Germans had demolished the harbor facilities, rendering it a hollow victory. Over the next seven weeks the Allies would fight a bitter battle for the *bocage* and the city of Caen, before finally breaking out of Normandy during Operation Cobra[4] in the last week of July.

THE BATTLEFIELD TODAY

Due to their dramatic history the Normandy beaches have become a popular tourist attraction, with many preserved artifacts. The drive through the Norman countryside is very picturesque and Normandy is accessible from the Channel ports or Paris. The area around the Normandy beaches is still rural, so the road network becomes restricted near the coast. There are numerous markers and orientation maps along the beach, although it is a good idea to obtain one of the many guidebooks available to better appreciate the significance of many of the locations. A good map is essential, as some of the more significant sites can be easily overlooked. In addition, some areas are privately owned and wandering tourists are not welcome. The landing areas at Omaha Beach stretch for about 7,000yds (3miles/5km) so the beach can be visited on foot in one day, depending on the amount of time spent at the many sites. The neighboring D-Day beaches are also within easy reach by car so if time is limited, it is useful to determine in advance which sites are of special interest. Some of the museums located near the other beaches are dedicated to the D-Day landings in general and should not be overlooked. For readers interested in uniforms and military equipment, many of these contain an interesting display of preserved artifacts. For example, the private "Musee Sous-Marins" at Commes contains one of the DD tanks recovered from offshore along with other equipment sunk on D-Day.

The toll of war. A temporary grave for one of the Rangers killed on Pointe-du-Hoc was created amongst the litter of war. (NARA)

One of the most impressive sites is Pointe-du-Hoc, which remains little changed from 1944, still pockmarked with bomb craters. The site has become overgrown with grass and weeds over the years, but the sense of the devastation there in 1944 is still obvious. Most of the concrete bunkers remain, cleaned up a bit and the debris removed. The view over the cliff is a vivid reminder of the courage of the Rangers. Pointe-du-Hoc is separated from the main landing beaches by the Pointe-et-Raz-de-la-Percée promontory and so is best reached by car before or after visiting the landing beaches. It is readily accessible from the coastal road (D.514).

Probably the best known of the sites at Omaha Beach is the US military cemetery located on the bluffs near St Laurent, and most ceremonies dedicated to the US forces on D-Day have been held here. More than 9,000

Reinforcement of the 1st Infantry Division sector began on the evening of 7 June with the arrival of the 2nd Infantry Division. Here we see a column moving up the bluff near the E-1 St Laurent draw on the morning of 8 June 1944. (MHI)

GIs are buried in the cemetery, mostly from the fighting after D-Day, and the row upon row of markers stand as a very tangible reminder of the cost of the Normandy campaign. There are numerous memorials located along and above the beach dedicated to units which took part in the D-Day landings or during later fighting in France.

The beach itself has seen many changes from 1944, since Normandy remains a popular seaside attraction in France. Most of the smaller beach obstructions have long since been cleaned away, although there are remains of the Mulberry harbor near the Vierville draw. Since the Vierville draw was the primary route from the Mulberry harbor off the beach, it was heavily reworked by US engineers in 1944, and so bears little resemblance to the defensive position of June 1944. The National Guard memorial was placed on the location of the 75mm gun casemate of the WN72 strongpoint. Some of the other draws are less important for access to the beach and so remain closer to their original condition. Many of the concrete casemates located in the draws are still in place, some of them dedicated as monuments to the fighting. The anti-tank gun casemate of the WN65 strongpoint shown in one of the photos has been preserved. Many of the bunkers and other shore fortifications have been removed or altered over the years. For example, none of the *Panzerstellung* turreted tank bunkers are still preserved, and other bunkers have been sealed up. Casual tourists should not wander into bunkers at Omaha Beach or elsewhere along the Normandy coast, except for those clearly intended for tourist visits. Many have ammunition sub-basements at the bottom of the access stairs that present a serious hazard to the unwary as the doors have often been removed or rotted away.

FURTHER READING

The D-Day landings have proven to be one of the most popular topics of World War II history, and there are hundreds of titles on this subject of varying quality. There was a flood of new books around the time of the 1994 anniversary. The list below is by no means exhaustive and consists mainly of more recent titles that the author has found to be particularly useful. Besides the commercially published books, there are a number of limited-circulation books by US Army commands that are particularly useful for those looking for more in-depth coverage, and can be found in specialist military libraries. The two most relevant are the First US Army and the V Corps report of operations. There are also many after-action reports on the D-Day landings that are more difficult to find except at archives. The author consulted the collections at the Military History Institute at the Army War College at Carlisle Barracks, Pennsylvania, and the US National Archives and Records Administration (NARA) at College Park, Maryland. Some of the better reports include the "Operation Report Neptune: Omaha Beach" by the Provisional Engineer Special Brigade Group, and "Amphibious Operations: Invasion of Northern France: Western Task Force June 1944" by the US Fleet HQ. There are also numerous after-action reports by the various US Army units located in Record Group 407 at NARA, College Park.

Stephen Ambrose, *D-Day, June 6, 1944* (Simon & Schuster, 1994). This account of the D-Day landings by the popular historian is based on many interviews with veterans that present the soldiers' perspectives of the fighting.

Joseph Balkoski, *Beyond the Beachhead: The 29th Infantry Division in Normandy* (Stackpole, 1989). This is an excellent account of the formation and training of the 29th Division and its actions in the Normandy campaign.

Sid Berger, *Breaching Fortress Europe* (Society of American Military Engineers, 1994). This book looks at the role of US Army engineer troops in the D-Day landings.

George Bernage, *Omaha Beach* (Heimdal, 2002). This is an excellent photographic portrayal of Omaha Beach on D-Day, and the best single volume detailing the configuration of the German beach defenses.

Joseph Ewing, *29 Let's Go!: A History of the 29th Division in World War II* (Infantry Journal 1948; Battery Press reprint 1979). This is one of the better semi-official divisional histories published immediately after the war with a very good account of the division at Omaha Beach.

Jonathan Gawne, *Spearheading D-Day* (Histoire & Collections, 1998). This is a superb, and lavishly illustrated examination of the US special units deployed during the Normandy landings with excellent coverage of their specialized equipment, and uniforms.

Gordon Harrison, *Cross-Channel Attack* (US Army CMH, 1951). This is the official US Army "Green Book" history of the Normandy landings and remains one of the best available accounts.

David Isby, *Fighting the Invasion: The German Army at D-Day* (Greenhill, 2000). This is the best single volume on the German army on D-Day and consists of a collection of essays written by senior German leaders for the US Army's Foreign Military Studies program after the war based on their recollections of the campaign.

Tim Kilvert-Jones, *Omaha Beach* (Leo Cooper, 1999). This is one of the popular Battleground Europe paperbacks combining a tour guide of the battlefield with an excellent short narrative of the battle.

H.R. Knickerbocker, et. al., *Danger Forward: The Story of the First Division in World War II* (1947, Battery Press reprint 2002). This is one of the better divisional histories published immediately after the war covering the division at the center of the US landings.

Adrian Lewis, *Omaha Beach: A Flawed Victory* (University of North Carolina, 2001). This is an excellent academic study of the planning of the D-Day landings.

Samuel E. Morison, *The Invasion of France and Germany 1944–1945* (Little, Brown, 1957). This is the volume in Morison's multi-volume history of the US Navy in World War II, and remains the best single account of US Navy actions on D-Day.

Omaha Beachhead (US Army CMH, 1945, numerous reprints) This is the earlier and shorter official history of the Omaha Beach landings, and is available in a paperback edition from the US Government Printing Office, including an excellent set of maps.

Winston Ramsey, *D-Day Then and Now, Volume 2* (After the Battle, 1995). This is a typically lavish and massive "After the Battle" treatment with an excellent selection of historical photos, complemented by photos of the same sites today.

Friedrich Ruge, *Rommel in Normandy* (Presidio, 1984). This is an account of Rommel's efforts in Normandy by his naval aide, and provides an inside view of the debates over German defensive strategy in 1944.

Paul Stillwell, *Assault on Normandy* (US Naval Institute, 1994). This is an excellent collection of essays by US Navy participants of the D-Day landings.

INDEX

Figures in **bold** refer to illustrations

air operations 23, 43, 46, 89, 90–1
  see also bombing and bombardment
air power, Europe 9, 10–11
aircraft, Marauders **23**
Allied forces
  air power 9, 10–11
  battle style 10–11
  command structure 16–17
  intelligence 11
  plans 21–30, **24**, **28**
  see also British Army; US Army; US
    Army Air Force; US Navy
amtracs (amphibious tractors) 27
Ancon, USS 80
anti-tank vehicles and weapons **32**, 34,
  36, 69, **70**, 84
Arkansas, USS **22**
artillery, German 36–7
  50mm PaK 38 anti-tank guns **32**, 34
  88mm PaK 43/41 "Scheunentor" **33**
  105mm leFH 18/40 **33**
  coastal guns 7, 14
  decoys **78**
  gun casemates **31**, **78**
  Omaha dispositions 33–5
  WWI field guns **89**
artillery, US **70**, 82–3, **85**
Atlantic Wall 14, 15
Augusta, USS **17**, **42**

beach defenses **10**, 13, **14**, 22, 30–8, **31**
  anti-tank ditches **83**
  clearing 80–2
  gun pits **32**
  trenches 34–5, **34**
Belgian gates 31
Bingham, Maj Sidney 55, 59, 63
bombing and bombardment
  air operations 23, 43, 46, 89, 90–1
  US Navy bombardment 22–3, 46,
    65–7, **65**, **71**, 89
Bradley, LtGen Omar 17–18, **17**, 30, 67, 69
British Army, Commandoes **72–4**, **79**
Bryant, Adm 65–6
bulldozers 25, 52, 63, **83**

Cabourg 63, 86
Canham, LtCol Charles "Stoneface"
  19–20, 55, 62, 84
Carmick, USS 66
casualties, German 89
casualties, US **50**, **81**, **82**, **83**, 87–9
  first and second wave 54, 59
  Gap Assault Teams 53
Charlie beach **47**, 80
Cointet gates 31

Colleville 66, 68, 87
Collins, J. Lawton 27
communications, German 68
communications, US 64, **65**, 79
Corlett, MajGen Charles 27
Cota, BrigGen Norman "Dutch" **19**, 20,
  55, **60–2**, 80

D-1 Vierville draw 46, **47**, 65, 80–1, 93
D-3 Les Moulins draw 34, **59**, **63**, **64**
  attacks on 50, 53, 54–5, 66, 81
destroyers **22**, 65–7, **65**
Dog Green beach 46, **47**, 50, 54, 80
Dog Red beach 46, 55, **60–2**
Dog White beach 53, 54, **87**
Dollman, Generaloberst Friedrich 15, 42
Doyle, USS 66
draws 33–4
  see also individual draws by name
Driscoll, Maj Edmond 18
DUKWs **55**, 82–3

E-1 St Laurent draw 51, 67, 81, **81**, **86**, 93
E-3 Colleville draw 9, 34, 66,**68**
  attacks on 52, 63, 81–2
  landings near 51, **66**, 67
Easy Green beach **59**, 81
Easy Red beach **31**, **59**
  clearing 80–1
  landings **6**, 47, 51, 67, **69**, **70**, 82
  operations 59–63
Eisenhower, Gen. Dwight D. 16–17, **17**,
  18, **19**, 22
Element C 31
Emmons, USS 66
equipment, US Army 21, **29**, 40

F-1 draw 52, 63
Fox Green beach 51, **52**, 63, **66**, **68**, 81
Fox Red beach 66

gas masks **29**
Gebelin, Lt Commander A.L. **22**
Gerhardt, MajGen Charles 19
German Air Force 11, 14, 35, **37**, 38, 90–1
German armed forces 36–8
  commanders and command structure
    13–16
  order of battle 38
  plans 30–5
  strategy 14–16
German Army
  1944 worldwide dispositions 10
  2/HKAA.1260 38
  Army Group B 14–15
  battle style 10–11
  commanders 13–16
  intelligence 11

Mobile Brigade 68, 84, 90
  Omaha dispositions **8**
  Panzers 15, 91
  prisoners of war **81**, **86**
German Army: 352nd Infantry Division
  33, 36–7, **36**, 84
  352nd Fusilier Battalion 37
  GR.914 37, 79–80, 84
  GR.915 37, 69, 85
  GR.916 37, 64, 68, 69, 75, 84
  I/AR.352 37
  II/AR.352 37
  Kampfgruppe Meyer 37, 43, 53, 64, 87, 90
German Army: 716th Infantry Division 30,
  36, 75
  GR.726 36, 37, 38, 68, 75–8, 84
  GR.726, 439th Ost Battalion 36
German Navy 14, 91
Gerow, MajGen Leonard 18, 19, 26, 67
Geyr von Schweppenburg, Gen Leo
  Freiherr 15
Gibbs, LtCol 18
Gold Beach 64, 68, 90
Göring, Reichsmarschall Hermann 13

Hall, Adm 22–3
"hedgehogs" 31
helmet markings **60–2**, **71**, **72–4**, **82**, **87**
Hemmkurven 31
Hicks, LtCol Herbert 18
Hiroshi, Oshima 11
Hitler, Adolf 10, 13, 14, 15, 91
Hoge, BrigGen William 19
Horner, LtCol Charles 18
Huebner, MajGen Clarence **17**, 18–19

insignia, Allied
  116th Infantry **60–2**
  British Commandoes **72–4**
  engineers **82**, **87**
  Rangers **60–2**, **71**
intelligence 11

Keitel, Generalfeldmarschall Wilhelm 13
Kirk, RearAdm Alan **17**
Kraiss, GenLt Dietrich 16, **16**, 37, 53, 64,
  68–9, 79, 84, 89–90
Krancke, Adm. Theodor 14

landing craft 27, 81
  crew **56–8**
  LCAs **71**
  LCIs 39, 55, 66–8
  LCI-554 68
  LCTs **55**, **82**
  LCT-30 68
  LCVPs **6**, 40, **42**, 43, 46, **56–8**, 68
  loading 40, 50, **56–8**

95

Lanker, Lt Albert 13
Le Garde Hameau 85
Le Havre, coastal guns **7**
life belts **21**

McCook, USS 65, 66
Marcks, General der Infanterie Erich
   15–16, 43
Marshall, George C. 16, 18
medical treatment 63, **81–3**
Meyer, Oberstlt 90
mines and mine clearance 31, 42, 80–2, **87**

Nivens, Coxswain D. 46, 47

OKW 13
Omaha Beach
   aerial views **9**, **47**, **90**
   cross-sectional view **21**
   geography 32–3
   reasons for selection 21
   see also beach defenses
Omaha Beach: operations
   aerial views **55**
   battlescenes **56–8**, **60–2**, **72–4**
   bird's eye views **44–5**, **48–9**, **76–7**
   landings **6**, **54**
Operation Anvil 7, 9
Operation Fortitude 9, 22
Operation Overlord 7–9
Operation Pointblank 9
Operation Swordhilt 27
orders of battle 38, 41
Organization Todt 13, 14, **30**

Parker, Lt Charles 55, 79
Pas de Calais 9, 11, 14
Pointe-du-Hoc 35, 38, **71**, **75**, **78**, 92
   operations at 22, 40, 43, 55, 70–80,
      72–4, **79**
   strategic importance 30
Pointe-et-Raz-de-la-Percée 9, 22, 33, 35,
   40, **47**, 65
Priller, Oberstlt Josef "Pips" 91

Raaen, Capt John 62
radios **65**
Raeder, Adm 13
ramp obstacles 31
rocket craft **23**
roller-grenades 33
Rommel, Erwin
   on air power 11
   and beach defenses **14**, 30–1, **31**, 89
   on D-Day 42
   responsibilities re western defenses 14–15
   and troop deployment 37
"Rommel's Asparagus" 31
Royce, Gen Ralph **17**
Rudder, LtCol James E. 20, 70, **79**
Rundstedt, Generalfeldmarschall Gerd
   von 13, 14

Saint Laurent 84
Samel Chase, USS 46, 47, 68
Satterlee, USS 71, 78
Saving Private Ryan (film) 51
Schwartz, Lt Stanley 62
signal lamps **79**

Spalding, Lt John 52
Sperrle, Generalfeldmarschall Hugo 14, 90
Streczyk, Sgt Philip 52
strongpoints 33–5
   WN60, capturing **52**, **53**, 63
   WN61 34, 52, 68
   WN62 34, 52
   WN63 63
   WN 64 63, 67
   WN65 64, 67, 81, 93
   WN66 34, 54, 55, **63**, 64, 66
   WN67 34, 64, 84
   WN68 34, 64, 66
   WN70 54, 64
   WN73 65
   WN76 90
Struble, RearAdm A.D. **17**

Talley, Col 80
tanks 24–9
   anti-tank vehicles and weapons **32**, 34,
      36, 69, **70**, 84
   British "Funnies" 24–6
   Churchills 25, 29
   dozer-tanks 25, 52, **83**
   landing 25–6, 46–50, 58
   losses 84
   M4 **87**
   M4A1 **6**, **56–8**, **67**, **68**, **85**
   M4A1 Duplex Drive amphibious 25–7,
      25
   M4A3E2 27–9
   operations 52, 54, 55–9, 63, 66, 84
   Panzers 15, 91
   wading trunks **25**, 26, **56–8**
Taylor, LtCol George **18**, 19, 63
Texas, USS 71, 80
Thompson, USS **22**
trenches **34**
trucks, amphibious 55, 82–3
Tschechenigel 31

uniforms and clothing
   British Commandoes **72–4**
   chemical-weapon protection 58
   US Army **21**, **27**, **72–4**
US Army 38–41
   1st Infantry Division **21**, **27**, 39
   2nd Infantry Division **93**
   29th Infantry Division 39
   81st Chemical Weapons Battalion **85**
   artillery battalions 82–3
   commanders 16–20
   Naval Shore Fire Control Parties **65**
   order of battle 41
   uniforms and equipment **21**, **27**, 40, **72–4**
US Army: 16th RCT (16th Infantry
   Regiment, 1st Infantry Division) **21**, **27**,
      40, **43**, 85
   1/116th **6**, **56–8**
   3/116th 59, 85
   741st Tank Battalion 39, 47–50, 52, 59,
      63, 68, 84
   741st Tank Battalion, Co. A 67, **85**
   Co. A 63
   Cos. E and F 51, 52
   Co. G 52, 59, 63, 85
   Co. I 51
   Co. L 51, **52**, **53**, 63

command post 63
commanders 18–19, **18**
Gap Assault Team activities 51–2
landing 51
objectives 29, 38–9
order of battle 41
US Army: 18th RCT (1st Infantry
   Division) 41, 67–8, **69**, **70**, 85
US Army: 26th RCT 41
US Army: 115th RCT (29th Infantry
   Division) 41, 67, 84
US Army: 116th RCT (116th Infantry
   Regiment, 29th Infantry Division)
   60–2, 84
   1/116th 51, 59–63
   2/116th 54
   3/116th 54–5, 63, 84
   743rd Tank Battalion 39, 46, 54, 59,
      66, 80, 84
   743rd Tank Battalion, Co. C 87
   Co. A 50–1
   Co. B 54
   Co. C 54, 55, 62
   Co. D 54
   Co. E 51
   Co. F 50
   Co. G 50, 55, 67
   Co. H 54, 59
   commanders 19, 20
   Gap Assault Team activities 53
   landing 50–1
   landing plans 24
   objectives 29, 39
   order of battle 41
US Army: 175th RCT 41
US Army: engineers (Engineer Special
   Brigades) 67, 80–2, **82**, 86, **87**
US Army: engineers (Gap Assault Teams)
   26, 29, 40, 51–3
US Army: Rangers
   2nd **29**, 40, 70–80, **71**, **72–4**, **79**
   2nd, Cos. A and B 54
   2nd, Co. C 50, 51
   5th 40, 54–5, **60–2**, 79, 84
   commanders 20
   equipment 40
   objectives 30, 39–40
US Army Air Force 10–11, 23, **23**, 89
US Navy, bombardment 22–3, 46, 65–7,
   65, 71, 89

Vierville 55, 84

Wall, Capt Herman 82
weapons **56–8**
   bangalore torpedoes **26**, **27**, **60–2**
   BARS **71**
   bazookas **27**, **71**
   charges **26**, **27**
   chemical, protection against **56–8**
   German 36–7
   "Goliath" **32**
   M1 carbines **27**
   Sten guns **72–4**
   water proofing **27**, **43**, **56–8**, **60–2**
Weymouth **29**, **71**
WN60-76 *see* strongpoints

Ziegelmann, Col Fritz 90